MW00474695

Praise for *Writing for Busy Readers*

"A home run. A must-read for everyone who communicates in writing."

—Robert Cialdini, author of *Influence: The Psychology of Persuasion*

"However skilled a writer you are, the insights and tools presented here will make you better. The techniques speak to both courtesy and strategy: respect readers' time, understand their needs, and you'll gain their focus and trust. Grounded in research but designed for impact."

—Nancy Gibbs, Harvard University, former managing editor of *Time* and coauthor of *The Presidents Club*

"Indispensable! This actionable, evidence-based guide will help you unleash the power of effective writing. Witty, well-organized, and imminently useful, *Writing for Busy Readers* is a gem. You'll never craft a subpar email, text, or memo again."

—Katy Milkman, Wharton School of the University of Pennsylvania, author of *How to Change*

"Amazing. The best book ever written on effective writing. It will change your life—and make the world a better place."

—Cass R. Sunstein, Harvard University, coauthor of *Nudge*

"Inspiring and practical in equal measure and successfully shows the profound difference that effective written communication can make. The contest for people's attention is fierce but we've all got a better chance with this book as our guide."

—Ros Atkins, BBC News

"Science-based tips to help you cut through the noise and reach readers. This is a helpful guide to achieving your communication goals."

—Viorica Marian, Northwestern University,
author of *The Power of Language*

"Cost: $28 and three hours of time. Benefit: Hundreds of hours of your time and thousands of hours of the time of others. Conclusion: Good deal."

—Max H. Bazerman, Harvard Business School,
author of *Complicit*

Writing *for* Busy Readers

COMMUNICATE
MORE EFFECTIVELY IN
THE REAL WORLD

Todd Rogers and
Jessica Lasky-Fink

An imprint of Penguin Random House LLC
penguinrandomhouse.com

City park image on pages 19, 20, 22, 126 by Macrovector/Shutterstock;
person cleaning dog poop icon on pages 117, 118 by popicon/Shutterstock;
outboard engine on pages 39, 109 by Vladyslav Horoshevych/Shutterstock;
spark plug on pages 39, 109 by Christian Delbert/Shutterstock;
butterfly ballot on page 163 from Reddit;
illustration on page 204 by Alexis Seabrook;
document icons on page 207 by porcelaniq/Shutterstock;
treasure chest icon on page 207 by Cube29/Shutterstock;
navigation icon on page 207 by keenani/Shutterstock;
tablet icon on page 207 by Blan-k/Shutterstock;
smartphone icon on page 207 by Blan-k/Shutterstock.

LIBRARY OF CONGRESS CATALOGING-IN-PUBLICATION DATA
has been applied for.

ISBN 9780593187487 (hardcover)
ISBN 9780593187494 (ebook)

Printed in the United States of America
2nd Printing

BOOK DESIGN BY TIFFANY ESTREICHER

For busy writers and readers everywhere

Contents

PART THREE

Putting the Principles to Work

Writing *for* Busy Readers

Introduction

This is a book we never planned to write.

There are already plenty of how-to books about the writing process. Nobody we know, ourselves included, would normally think to read a book about writing. There is also something peculiar about the very concept of writing about writing. It seems circular and self-referential: "Writing about writing" sounds a lot like, say, "singing about singing." Then gradually, almost without our noticing, we became convinced that there is a genuine need for a different kind of book about writing—one that explains, point by point, the proven techniques for communicating effectively with any recipient, any reader. We also recognized a need to focus specifically on the *busy* reader, because we live in an unprecedented age of media saturation and information overload. Modern writers need extra help breaking through all the distractions.

What you will read about in these pages draws on a vast body of research, much of it by us. It is also informed by many years of our professional and personal experiences. Todd spent a decade working on the science of writing to busy voters. Both of us worked on the science of writing to busy families. During the pandemic, we advised state and local leaders on how to write to busy constituents. Step by step, we realized that some principles of effective writing are nearly universal and yet are not well-known.

Viewed this way, the analogy with singing carries a quite different message. Singing is a simple thing that anyone can do but that most of us don't do particularly well. Great singers learn not just by listening to others and making subjective, aesthetic judgments. They train and improve by following well-developed techniques that are grounded in objective studies of anatomy, acoustics, and human perception. So it is with writing.

Today, we know what goes on inside a busy reader's brain. We know how a reader's eyes move as they respond to different stimuli. We know why certain types of writing draw a reader's focus while others tend to get lost in the fog of distraction and competition for attention. We wrote this book to share these important, potentially life-changing insights. It is a guide to the science of writing so busy people read and respond.

THE PATH FROM IDEA TO ACTION

The principles of this book apply to everyone, because we are all writers.

More and more of our lives are conducted via text, email, and other digital messages. All of that is layered on top of the older types of practical writing such as office reports, school updates, registration forms, newsletters, and notifications. These types of practical communications generally ask readers to perform a task or to engage with a piece of information. Sometimes we want readers to understand details about upcoming plans, vaccination schedules, disclosures, or policy changes. Other times we need readers to take action, like providing feedback, answering a question, completing a form, or scheduling a meeting.

You may not think of yourself as a writer, but consider this: Has a day ever gone by when you didn't write anything? A text message is writing. A work email is writing. A Facebook post or a tweet is writing. An update on Slack is writing. Even a to-do list on the fridge is a form of writing—in this case, a message to your future, busy self. All of those things are more effective if they are written in ways that account for how busy people read. Such communications are pretty much inescapable in modern life, which is why we say that *we are all writers.* Equally important, *we are all readers, too.* We wear both hats. And these days, most of us are *busy* readers, faced with many conflicting demands for our time.

Effective writing makes life easier, more pleasant, and more productive both for the writer and for the reader. It is a power—an almost magical power that can transmit a thought or goal from your head into someone else's head, and then inspire them to act in response. It breaks through the cloud of distraction that surrounds busy people. And it is something that anyone can do. Once you learn the principles behind effective writing, that power is yours.

This book will set out the six fundamental principles of effective writing and provide guidance on how to put them to work. But first, we want to be clear about what effective writing is, and why it is such an important but misunderstood skill.

- *Effective writing has a well-defined purpose.* Writing is how you share ideas that are important to you. It is also how you convince other people to do what you want them to do, whether that means reading a memo, picking the restaurant where you'll have lunch, or signing up to volunteer at a community event. Effective writing gets through to the reader, even the busy reader whose own goal may be to stop reading and move on as quickly as possible. If you lose your reader, it's not their fault; it is your job as the writer to capture their attention and keep them engaged.

- *Effective writing helps the writer as well as the reader.* Most of us write for practical reasons dozens, maybe hundreds, of times each week. So we must be good at it, right? Turns out, we're far worse at practical writing than we think we are. Too often, our messages go unanswered. We get late or incomplete responses. Seemingly simple exchanges become complicated and confusing. The principles of effective writing help you get your point across more clearly and quickly so that things happen when you want them to.

Being clear with your words also forces you to be clear in your own thinking. It brings your ideas and goals into sharper focus.

- *Effective writing is not the same as beautiful writing.* Expressive, literary writing is a time-honored craft, but a highly subjective one that can take a lifetime to master. It is often consumed as a form of recreation by people who have the time and who have already decided to set aside other tasks so that they can indulge themselves in their reading. Often, beautiful writing is intentionally demanding and multilayered. Effective writing, on the other hand, is a skill that anyone can master, and it has a very specific goal: clearly convey specific information to busy people and make it easy for them to understand and respond.

- *There is a rigorous science underlying the rules of effective writing.* We can argue endlessly about what kind of writing is most beautiful, but effective writing is not so subjective. There are well-defined strategies, based on the science of human cognition, that offer guidance on how to be more effective writers. We have looked at hundreds of scientific studies and conducted our own research to see what works. We also draw lessons from our two careers as writers and communicators. This book codifies all of that knowledge into a set of principles designed to be applicable to all forms of practical communication.

- *Effective writing is read in a context.* Our six principles of effective writing (and the rules of application associated with each of them) can help anyone become a more effective writer and communicate more clearly with a busy reader. The underlying science is the same in every situation. How to put the principles into action will depend heavily on context, however. Each writer has a different voice and life experience; each reader has different expectations, assumptions, and biases. In each section of the book we will discuss the contextual considerations that we all face in the real world.

BETTER LIVING THROUGH EFFECTIVE WRITING

When was the last time you waited days (or weeks, months . . .) for a response to an important email you sent? We've all been there. Everyone is busy and, consciously or not, busy people are always weighing where and how to spend their limited time. Now think about the last dense, multiparagraph email you received. How much time did you spend reading it? For most of us, the answer is just a few seconds, if we attempted to read it at all. Busy people tend to skim, postpone reading complex messages, or ignore them entirely.

Ineffective writing can lead to real-world problems. Sometimes it is a matter of missed opportunity. In December 2020, Airbnb made its public debut on the stock market. Prior to going public, all Airbnb hosts received an email invitation to buy stock.[1] The email invitation was sent with the seemingly mundane and unimportant subject line "Airbnb's Directed Share Program." Many hosts reported ignoring or setting aside the email because it didn't seem especially urgent. The ones who read the email and took advantage of the opportunity made over $15,000. Airbnb and its hosts learned the hard way that messages are likely to go unread when written without a keen focus on how busy readers read.

As writers, however, it's easy to forget this harried reality. When we write, we too often believe our readers will find our messages as important to them as they are to us, and will allocate their attention accordingly.

Ineffective writing can also obscure personally important information, such as news about changes in the company healthcare plan or an opportunity to volunteer at a child's school fair. The average person receives dozens or even hundreds of messages—emails, text messages, and so on—each day, and the average professional spends nearly one-third of their workweek reading and responding to emails.[2] Those numbers don't even account for all the other communications that professionals receive outside the workplace. For busy readers, handling this torrent of information and messages is like living in an endless game of Whac-A-Mole. Highly relevant updates about health and school can inadvertently get overlooked or whacked with the delete button.

Even when ineffectively written communications *are* read, they impose an unkind tax on readers' time. At an event we recently led on this topic, one participant wrote: "Lengthy emails in today's work environment [are] disrespectful of the reader." The longer the message, the larger the tax. Imagine if you receive 120 emails every day (as many people do), and each is three paragraphs long. Reading them in their entirety would require four hours each day. Or flip the situation around and imagine you are sending a three-paragraph message to all 120 employees at your organization. You deliberate over every word; your high school English teacher would be so proud of you. But then it takes each employee two minutes on average to read what you wrote. Across 120 employees, your lovingly crafted message will impose a four-hour time tax. If you cut its length by just one paragraph, you would save eighty total minutes of employees' time.

And it gets worse: Ineffective writing can deter all readers, but especially readers who have limited literacy, who speak English as a second language, who have learning disabilities, who have limited time due to multiple jobs and challenging personal circumstances, or who face other significant barriers to reading and understanding written communications. In short, effective writing is more accessible, more equitable, and more democratic.

In the United States, electoral ballot initiatives often use complex, unclear language, such as this 2016 Colorado ballot question:[3]

> *Shall there be an amendment to the Colorado constitution concerning the removal of the exception to the prohibition of slavery and involuntary servitude when used as punishment for persons duly convicted of a crime?*

Does a *yes* vote on this initiative mean we endorse using slavery as punishment, or not? (We believe *yes* means we oppose using slavery as a punishment—but, honestly, it's hard to be sure.) Now imagine how hard this would be for voters who speak English as a second language, who have lower literacy skills, or who simply don't have the time to read and reread and re-reread the question before casting their ballots.

Many people would probably just give up on the question rather than attempt to figure out what it's asking. This is exactly what a 2011 study found: Voters are more likely to skip ballot questions that use more complex language.[4] Ineffective writing doesn't just decrease the chance people will respond to your emails. It can even pose serious problems for the legitimacy of electoral outcomes.

HOW TO USE THIS BOOK

In keeping with our own advice and guidance, we have structured this book to be as direct and effective as possible for you, the busy reader. To get the most out of it, though, we encourage you to think about your own goals as a writer and to understand what this book is designed to do.

In school we were taught the fundamentals of formal writing, including proper grammar, spelling, punctuation, and prose. Those of us raised in the American school system began learning about organization and flow, word choice, and voice in elementary school. In high school, we were taught the art of the five-paragraph essay and crafting thesis statements. These are critical skills, but much of the formal writing we learned in school is irrelevant or counterproductive for real-world practical writing.

As a result, most of us learn practical writing informally. We pick up strategies here and there by observing that some messages receive prompt responses, and for others we continue to wait for responses. Proper grammar and punctuation, full sentences, and appropriate word choice are almost always useful.

But if you email your company's leadership team a five-paragraph essay about how a client meeting went, they are unlikely to read it, no matter how beautiful the prose. These dueling styles—formal writing and practical writing—coexist uncomfortably in our heads, and most of us have never been trained how to combine them into *effective writing*.

In this book, you will not find recycled lessons on how to write well, à la the classic book *The Elements of Style* by Strunk and White. You also will not find simplistic, inflexible lists of writing rules, as you will find in some of the more modern how-to books on efficient (rather than effective) writing. Rather, our principles derive from the sciences of psychology and human behavior, blended with a social understanding that most people have limited time and attention.

Effective writing reflects an understanding of the science of how busy readers interact with our writing. This book is written with that interaction in mind. To distill the science, we have reviewed research in cognitive psychology, social psychology, behavioral economics, neuroscience, communications, literacy, teaching and learning, marketing, time management, and more. We've also conducted hundreds of randomized experiments with collaborators to understand what works and what doesn't.

Randomized experiments start with a large group of people. In a typical experiment, some people are randomly selected to receive a standard message (they are the "control group"), while others are randomly selected to receive the standard message plus a specific revision or modification (they are the "treatment group"). We then observe what fraction of each group does whatever the message was designed to prompt them to do: reply, click on a link, show up at an event, donate, and so on. By randomly selecting which participants receive each message, we can isolate the effect of the specific revision on the behavior. All the guidance we offer in this book comes from these types of studies. Note, however, that randomized experiments can provide only a broad snapshot of human behavior. They reveal tendencies over groups but cannot predict individual behavior. That said, they are highly valuable tools, the gold standard in research for helping us understand what works in the real world.

As we completed this book, we couldn't help applying some of these psychological insights to ourselves. We often joke that we decided the best way to help people write shorter, more effective messages was to write a whole book about it. We worked hard to keep this book as concise as possible, but we found that a full understanding could not be conveyed in just a short enumeration of our six core principles. Recognizing this seeming irony, we structured our book to be easy to navigate for busy readers who want to skip around—although we suggest you read it straight through.

However you approach this book, we hope it teaches useful skills as well as the illuminating science underlying them. Writing effectively helps writers achieve their goals. And our goal for this book is to help you achieve yours, in everything you write.

PART ONE

Engaging the Reader

1

Get Inside Your Reader's Head

"Why Is Everyone So Busy? Time Poverty Is a Problem Partly of Perception and Partly of Distribution"
—*The Economist*[1]

"Too Busy to Notice You're Too Busy"
—*The New York Times*[2]

"Why You Never Seem to Have Enough Time"
—*The Washington Post*[3]

Do you know that feeling of not having enough hours in the day? Of course you do. Everybody does. In a 2018 survey conducted by the Pew Research Center, 60% of adults—and 74% of parents—in the US reported that they feel too busy to enjoy life at least some of the time.[4] Those findings are consistent with our own studies, in which 60% of respondents said they often don't have enough time to get everything done in a typical month.[5] When we feel pressed for time, we typically try to do many things at once. But our attempts at multitasking can end up adding even more stress, anxiety, and fatigue.

To be an effective writer, we need to remember that our readers experience the scarcity of time every bit as acutely as we do. Their distractions influence both what they read and how they read it. To understand how to write for a busy reader, therefore, we need to understand what goes on inside a busy brain.

All of us have limited time, so we have to make constant trade-offs—especially when we're busy. Spending more time on one thing necessarily means spending less time on something else. We can respond to the dozen unread emails in our inboxes or we can go to the gym, but we can't do both. Or we can strike an unsatisfying compromise, getting to half of our unread emails and squeezing in half a workout. The relentless competition for our time affects our ability to engage with communications we receive.

Not only do we have limited time, we also have limited attention. Our finite mental capacity constrains the way we navigate the world. We may try to convince ourselves that we can actively focus on lots of things at the same time (the two of us tried it ourselves while we were writing this book), but it's a lie. Our attention is inherently limited. A classic study by the psychologist George Miller confirms that there is a distinct cap to how many specific things we can actively hold in our minds at once: approximately seven items, plus or minus two.[6]

Most of the time we're blissfully unaware of our cognitive limits. Think about what happens when you are driving down a busy city street. There are many overlapping details you need to pay attention to simultaneously to avoid an accident (and a ticket): stoplights, other cars, pedestrians, bikers, nearby sirens, the speed limit, potholes, traffic laws, and much more. When you're learning to drive, navigating all these obstacles requires an immense amount of attention and focus. But with practice, the processes become so automatic that most adults are able to drive even in the busiest cities without much conscious effort.

Yet studies show that multitasking makes even the most experienced drivers worse: the "distracted driver" phenomenon. Some psychologists have suggested that talking on the phone while driving has as bad an effect as being legally drunk while driving.[7] This inability to juggle tasks may seem odd, given that most US adults are both experienced drivers *and* experienced phone-talkers. Shouldn't both tasks come easily? Why can't our brains handle doing two familiar things at the same time?

The answer comes back to the constraints on our attention. Brain researchers have identified multiple types of attention. For our purposes here, "attention" is the mental process that notices what's going on and directs and focuses our limited cognitive resources.[8] The brain's attention system is what directs us to do things like notice ambulance sirens while we're driving, focus intently during a class lecture, or read and respond to an urgent work email. The brain's processing capacity is limited, which means that our attention system also has limits.

The limited capacity of our busy brains has three implications, each of which profoundly influences how we interact with the world around us, including what and how we read:

- We cannot notice or process everything in front of us.
- We can exhaust our focus over time, often in less time than we think.
- We struggle focusing on multiple things at one time, but we still try.

WHAT WE NOTICE—AND WHAT WE DON'T

At any given moment, we are typically confronted with more information than our brains can process. That holds true whether we're driving through a busy city, watching a live concert, or sitting in a work meeting on Zoom. The brain's attention system helps us navigate this overload by acting as a filter: It selects what information to notice and focus on and what information to suppress or exclude entirely from our awareness.[9] As we drive through a city, for instance, our attention system helps us notice traffic dangers by filtering out everything else happening around us; while you are behind the wheel, you are unlikely to notice people shopping, sidewalk conversations, and so on.

Life would be completely overwhelming if the attention system wasn't so limited. To keep the world manageable, our brains constantly evaluate all the types of information that bombard us (including sights, sounds, physical senses, emotions, and thoughts) and select what is important or relevant enough to make it through the filter. The selection process can happen unconsciously or it can be purposeful, allowing us to direct it. Right now, your attention system may be surreptitiously filtering out background noise or activity to help you read this sentence. But if someone calls your name in the next room, your selective attention will likely direct you to them and away from this sentence.

For readers, selective attention also guides what they visually notice and focus on when interacting with any kind of writing.[10] To see how selective attention works, glance at the following picture quickly before going on to the next paragraph.[11]

What did you notice first? Maybe it was the playground, the family of four sitting on the blanket on the bottom right, the car, or one of the bicyclists. Whatever your answer, it was the result of your selective visual attention at work. The brain can't immediately notice and process all the visual information in a detailed picture like this, so it uses shortcuts. The shortcuts used may vary depending on the person, the time, and the context. But there are two near-universal shortcuts you should be aware of.

Shortcut #1: We most quickly notice elements that have a strong visual contrast with their surroundings. See for yourself. What do you notice first in the modified version of the image on the next page?

You probably looked right away at the person walking their dog in the middle of the image. It automatically captures the brain's attention, because it visually contrasts with the rest of the scene. The same thing happens when you look into the night sky and notice a full moon even without trying. Our brains have evolved to automatically notice things that stand out from their surroundings. This is a basic feature of vision across many species. It has been documented in animals ranging from human infants[12] to barn owls.[13] And it has powerful implications for how readers approach written communications.

Shortcut #2: Our selective attention can be intentionally and purposefully directed. Return to the first picture on page 19, and this time try to find the *person sitting on the bench*. You probably didn't randomly cast your gaze back and forth across the image. Most likely, you started by scanning the walkway area for benches and then easily found the bench that has a person sitting on it. If you look really closely, you can see that they have a tiny dog on a leash with them, too. When we look for something specific, our attention system helps us efficiently and quickly find it.

However, in the process of noticing some elements, we miss others—often without realizing it. In the three times you've looked at the image, have you noticed the stack of four hexagonal shapes and a triangle that form a play structure in the left corner of the playground? We didn't see it the first few times we looked at this image, and we suspect you did not, either. It is even more visually prominent than the person sitting on the bench, but you probably did not note anything that made it worthy of your selective attention (until now, that is). As a result, it is in the scene, unnoticed, hidden in plain sight.

Brain research has revealed that when you notice and examine one item in a visual scene, the brain actively suppresses noticing other items that are also present.[14] As a result, we often don't notice the things we're not looking for. The brain's natural tendency to zero in on relevant information is an important fact for effective writing.

WHERE WE FOCUS

Once our selective attention helps us notice something noteworthy—whether it's a thing we see, hear, or read—the brain's attention system then helps us direct and manage the way we focus our mental resources on it.[15]

Let's continue the exercise and return to the first image. How many trees do you see?

You likely looked at the picture, used your visual attention to home in on the trees, and then focused your mental energy on systematically counting them. (The correct answer is six.) When necessary, our brains can remain focused on a task until completion—even a task as boring as counting trees in an image for no apparent reason. Focusing requires a lot of brainpower, however. That is especially true when we're focusing on a complicated or difficult task. Because of our brains' limited processing capacity, we can't focus on everything at once. Just as with noticing, our attention system has to be selective about what it focuses on and for how long.

While you were focusing on counting trees, you almost certainly were not counting the total number of people riding bicycles, scooters, and skateboards. That information was not relevant to the task at hand, so your brain ignored it, much as selective attention prevented you from noticing the hexagons-and-triangle play structure in the playground. The brain's ability to ignore irrelevant information can be almost comically intense. In a widely cited 1999 study, two Harvard researchers asked participants to focus their attention on counting how many times a basketball was passed back and forth in a one-minute video.[16] Halfway through the video, a person wearing a gorilla costume strolled directly through the scene. Nearly half of the people who watched the video failed to notice the sauntering gorilla.

Focusing helps us avoid mental overload, but it can also deplete our attention system. When we focus on one task for a long period of time or particularly intensely, our ability to stay focused declines. That is one of the reasons why schoolchildren get recess and writers take breaks: Directing and controlling our attention is difficult and tiresome. It doesn't require a long day of school or intense work to exhaust the resources of our attention system. The brain can run down more rapidly than you might expect.

In an illustrative study, psychologist Brandon Schmeichel and his colleagues asked a group of participants to watch a six-minute video of a person being interviewed.[17] At the same time, irrelevant words flashed across the screen. Half of the participants were told to avoid looking at the irrelevant words, while the other half were free to focus on whatever they wanted. The brain's selective attention is automatically inclined to focus on the flashing words (partly because they contrast prominently with their surroundings), so ignoring them required effortful focus and control.

The researchers then tested how much participants had been worn down by the use of their attentional focus, measuring their performance on two later tasks unrelated to the video. The first task was a long, difficult reading-comprehension test used for graduate school admissions. Participants who had been asked to control their attention by actively ignoring the flashing words on the video scored a significant 20% lower on the test than those who had not been asked to do so. Evidently, the earlier video task had exhausted the participants' focus, reducing how carefully they were able to read the essays and answer challenging questions.

Our ability to focus our attention is also affected by how we feel *physically*. This is different from the depletion of our brain's attention systems. When we are physically tired, it's systematically harder to focus. As most of us know all too well, we tend to lose concentration at the end of a long day, after a long workout, or after getting too little sleep.[18] Even well-trained athletes experience impaired attention and decision-making from physical exhaustion.[19]

Distractions and interruptions pose yet another challenge to our efforts to stay focused. Even with an open schedule and insatiable curiosity, few people would be able to read this book cover to cover in a single sitting. Our minds wander. It can readily happen even when reading something as short as a text message or a Facebook post. One recent study estimated that people's minds wander one-third of the time while they are trying to read. And be aware: Mind wandering happens even more frequently when we are reading complicated writing.[20]

Once we get distracted, it is hard to refocus. According to information scientist Gloria Mark at the University of California, Irvine, workers need an average of twenty-three minutes to return fully to a task after being interrupted.[21] Needless to say, this affects how well we do whatever it is we're doing. Another study, conducted at Carnegie Mellon University, found that being interrupted by a phone call while taking a reading test decreased performance on the test by 20%.[22] Writing effectively for busy people requires keeping in mind just how easily they (and we, all of us) can get worn down and distracted.

HOW WE JUGGLE TASKS

The brain's limitations in noticing and focusing inevitably translate into limitations in acting, as well. No matter how appealing the idea may seem, multitasking—doing multiple things at the same time—is no solution to the problem of having too much to do and too little time and attention to do it. Strictly speaking, it's not even possible to be thinking about two tasks at the exact same time. What we are actually doing when we are "multitasking" is switching rapidly between individual tasks, which is a cognitively costly process. As we switch back and forth, we are slower and more likely to miss important things than when we are tackling just one task at a time. Bouncing from task to task also depletes our focus more quickly. This is not a new insight. In the first century BCE, Publilius Syrus, a Latin writer, wrote that "to do two things at once is to do neither."[23] Modern research comes to a similar conclusion: When we attempt multiple tasks at once, we become less efficient at all of them.[24]

Despite this, we (the authors) keep trying to multitask, hoping we will come out ahead. And we are not alone. One survey of professionals found that 63% report regularly working on two or three different tasks at the same time.[25] In surveys we've conducted ourselves, about 50% of respondents report "often" multitasking in the prior week.[26]

Multitasking—or, more precisely, task switching—has an essential place in helping us negotiate our busy and complicated worlds. With limited time, our lives are easier if we can stir the pasta while seasoning the sauce, setting the table, and answering homework questions from our children. But we don't try to do many tasks at the same time solely because we're busy; we also multitask because we think we're better at it than we are. The bottom line is that your mind works most effectively when it has a clear anchor point: one thing it is noticing, one thing it is focusing on, one task that it needs to initiate in response. Writing that respects those limitations is more likely to get through to a busy brain—and to the reader who possesses it.

To simulate how hard it is to focus (effectively) on two tasks at the same time, try out another experiment on yourself. Say out loud the kind of formatting that has been applied to each of the following words:

italicize
bold
CAPITALIZE
<u>underline</u>
highlight

Now, again say out loud the kind of formatting applied to each of the following words:

highlight
italicize
BOLD
underline
capitalize

You probably discovered that, compared to the first set of words, the second set required significantly more effort, took more time, and may have induced an error or two. This is called the Stroop effect. It illustrates how difficult it is to focus on even two cognitive tasks at the same time.[27] Identifying the formatting requires focused attention on the letters, and in the process we read the words themselves without trying to. When the written words are consistent with the formatting applied to the words (e.g., "*italicize*"), the activity is relatively easy and quick. But when the written words are inconsistent with the formatting (e.g., "italicize"), the activity is much harder.

The second list can be almost painful to read and describe. That is the Stroop effect in action. When the written words and the formatting applied to the words are consistent, there's only one cognitive task: Both identifying the kind of formatting and speaking its name are one and the same. But when the words and formatting are inconsistent, the brain now has to deal with two cognitive tasks: There is still the main task of identifying and saying the name of the formatting, but now there's the second task of effortfully suppressing the impulse to say the word that was read.

The mental clashes created by multitasking (or, more accurately, rapid task-switching) can have serious real-life consequences. A team from Butler University and Eli Lilly found that pharmacists who were asked to answer questions while doing their work took longer and made substantially more errors completing prescriptions. Multitasking slowed them down and caused them to miss critical details.[28] Texting while driving might be even more deadly. US government statistics attribute thousands of road deaths each year to this dangerous habit.[29] Yet, by some estimates, 22% of drivers report doing this type of multitasking daily.[30]

This is the landscape of stress and distraction that you are entering every time you write something intended for a busy reader—which are nearly all readers, these days. Effective writing respects the innate limitations of the busy brain, making it both useful and also *kind*, because it minimizes the stress you are placing on the reader.

2

Think Like a Busy Reader

Once you have a deeper insight into what goes on inside a reader's brain, you can appreciate the immense challenge of breaking through all that clutter and noise. Fortunately, you don't have to guess how to go about it! We have drawn on a large body of professional experience and academic research (along with personal insights) to provide proven guidance.

The first step to writing effectively is understanding the ways in which limited time and attention affect how busy people read. Then you can begin to work your way past the fundamental hurdles that determine whether an idea in your head will find a home in someone else's head: the filters that decide whether, when, and how carefully to read the messages they receive.

Every time a reader encounters a written communication—even something as short as an email, a text, a Slack message, or a social media post—they go through a four-stage process:

- First, they must decide whether to engage with it at all.
- Second, if they decide to engage, they then must decide when to engage. Sometimes the decision to engage leads to a decision to engage later.
- Third, once they do engage, they must decide how much time and attention to allocate to reading the message.
- Fourth, if they read something that requires a response, they must decide whether to respond or react.

These decisions are often nearly instantaneous, performed with little or no conscious thought. Rarely do we carefully deliberate about each stage. But a tremendous amount of mental processing happens during that tiny blip of time. Our job as effective writers is to navigate each of the four critical rounds in that brief but daunting process.

DECIDING WHETHER TO ENGAGE

When readers receive a communication, they automatically put it to a test: Is this message worth my time? Should I even bother engaging with it?

Economists describe this type of decision-making as "expected utility maximization." When making decisions between alternatives, people weigh the expected costs and benefits of all possible choices; then they choose the option that maximizes the expected benefits and minimizes the expected costs. People consider their time precious, so the threshold to engage can be quite high. In a recent survey we conducted with around 1,800 working professionals, they estimated that they delete about half of the emails they receive without reading them.[1]

That is a striking result when you think about it from a cognitive perspective. Busy readers routinely decide how valuable a message is *without actually reading it*! And working professionals are hardly the only ones making snap judgments based on limited information. We all do the same basic thing, all the time, using mental shortcuts that simplify decision-making.

Decision researchers call these mental shortcuts "heuristics," but for simplicity, we'll call them "rules of thumb." One common rule of thumb is that, when faced with a lot of options, we pick the first one that seems good enough (sometimes called "satisficing"), rather than expending the effort to seek out the absolute best measured option. Think about how many movies are available on Netflix. It would take days to search through every available option to find the one that will maximize your enjoyment. The "good enough" rule allows you to cut the task down to a minute or two. Rules of thumb help us navigate complex, information-rich decisions—from choosing Netflix shows to sorting through our email inbox.

Readers often infer the value of a communication from its "envelope," the readily available information surrounding a communication that signals its content.[2] For an email, this information might be the sender or subject line. For an office memo, it might be the title. For a traditional letter, it might be the return address or the format of the physical envelope. (In essence, we really do judge a book by its cover.) Readers read these clues and then apply rules of thumb to determine whether to engage. We might prioritize messages from someone we are close to, such as a friend or family member. Conversely, we might choose to ignore messages from senders we don't recognize, especially if the rest of the available cues make those messages appear irrelevant.

Estimating the expected *benefits* of a received message is only half of the calculation that busy readers make when deciding whether to engage with a communication. They also consider the *costs* involved: How much time and effort will be required to engage? Here, too, people apply rules of thumb to make this assessment. Their initial estimate of costs (measured in both time and effort) heavily influences readers' decisions to engage. Most notably, they are more likely to engage with messages that are short or that appear easy to navigate because they seem like they will require less time, attention, and effort to read.

The preference for short, easy messages makes obvious sense, but busy readers with too little time and attention can also be myopic, sometimes even illogical: They tend to heavily prioritize the present over the future. Have you ever decided that next week you'll start saving money or dieting or exercising? And then when next week arrived, you decided that you would really start . . . the *next* week? Yeah, we do it, too. Most of us prefer doing enjoyable, pleasant, easy, and gratifying things now and push off less pleasant, more difficult things until later. Even though the ultimate cost of those will be just the same, it feels like we are coming out ahead by not paying the cost right now.

DECIDING WHEN TO ENGAGE

Revisiting the Netflix question from a cost perspective, imagine that you have narrowed down the vast set of movie offerings to just a couple options. How do you choose which one to watch right now? The movies we want to watch often fall into two categories. There are the ones we *want* to watch because we think they'll be enjoyable, such as entertaining action movies or romantic comedies, and the ones we feel like we *should* watch because we think they'll be educational or good for us, like award-winning documentaries or foreign-language films.

Research that we conducted with our colleagues has shown that people tend to watch the more enjoyable movies first, before getting around to the "good for us" options.[3] Other studies have examined "want" versus "should" decisions in professional contexts and confirmed that people tend to procrastinate before turning to tasks that are more difficult and less enjoyable.[4] When people are asked to complete a mixed set of easy and hard tasks, they typically tackle the easy tasks first. The pattern holds true even if people are offered financial incentives for prioritizing the hard ones.[5]

In fact, sometimes we are even willing to pay a price in order to enjoy pleasant things right now. A classic study asked people whether they would prefer to receive "$100 right now" or "$101 in one week." Most people chose the desirable thing (receiving $100 right now), even though it meant forgoing a slightly more desirable thing in the near future.[6] Getting an extra 1% in one week is equivalent to earning 68% interest over one year, yet participants in the experiment typically decided they'd rather not wait one week for the additional money.

Just as we forgo benefits to have good things now, we are also willing to incur costs to push unpleasant things off until later. In one of our student surveys, participants reported that they would rather sit in traffic for thirty-one minutes a week from now than sit for thirty minutes right now, even knowing that postponing will end up costing them an extra minute of unpleasantness.[7] If you write something that your intended reader thinks is going to be an unpleasant slog, you can bet that they are going to put off reading it until . . . later.

The tendency to privilege the present over the future is hardwired into us. Researchers using magnetic resonance imaging (MRI) scans observed that particular parts of the brain associated with immediate rewards (the limbic reward-related regions) activate when we consider options that include desirable outcomes *now* but stay mostly dormant when considering options that only include desirable outcomes *later*.[8] Similar behavior has been observed across the human development cycle and even across different animal species, including rats, chimpanzees, and birds, to name a few.[9]

All of these cost-benefit calculations relate directly to the ways in which we engage with communications we receive. Busy readers are likely to prioritize messages they think can be dealt with easily and quickly, because they seem more enjoyable (or at least less awful). Conversely, readers tend to avoid messages that appear long and time-consuming, pushing them off into the future. Our surveys clearly show these responses: In one instance, a full 99% of working professionals in a class we taught said they would respond first to a message that they perceived to be easier to deal with than to one that appeared more difficult.[10]

DECIDING HOW TO ENGAGE

Spoiler alert: *Everyone skims.*

Busy readers aim to extract as much value as possible from a communication with as little time and attention as possible. To achieve this, they don't always read linearly, line by line. They vary how they read to suit their goals. They may closely read one section, skim another, and jump around in yet another, searching for specific information that they consider relevant. In the language of economics theory: Busy readers maximize their expected utility by continuously trying to predict whether the value of spending another second reading the message is greater than the benefit of spending that time and attention on something else.

Readers don't intentionally think, "Okay, time to maximize my expected utility!" We simply move on when we get bored or distracted. Our conscious focus is constantly at risk of distraction. We can learn a lot of valuable information in the first few seconds spent reading a message, but soon we reach the point of diminishing returns—at least, that is our common expectation. Each additional second of our attention tends to yield less information, especially once we have surmised the gist of the message. From then on, our reading time becomes progressively less valuable. Busy readers have a low threshold for moving on: As soon as the expected value of the next second spent reading is lower than the value of whatever else we would be doing instead, we stop.

In general, reading for utility is an efficient strategy for extracting as much information as possible while expending as little time and attention as possible. But there's a problem: The value of some messages may be realized only if they're read in full. The whole may be greater than the sum of the individual parts.

Think about an email you might receive from a friend recounting a humorous encounter he had while at a Philadelphia Eagles football game. He was in the parking lot outside Lincoln Financial Field, eating hoagies and catching up with friends. An older couple walked by and struck up a conversation about the Eagles' defensive players and whether they were good enough to win the championship that year. After a few minutes, just as your friend was about to head into the stadium, he realized that the older couple were your parents, who by chance were visiting from Arizona that week. Out of sixty-five thousand fans there, what are the odds? If you had stopped reading the second you understood the gist of the message—that your friend went to a Philadelphia Eagles game—you would have missed the twist ending, which, really, was the entire point of the message.

Skimming also leaves readers vulnerable to misssing key information. Did you notice that "missing" was misspelled in the previous sentence? If you did, you were likely reading closely, which we appreciate—thank you! Close reading means you won't miss as much, but it also requires a lot more of your time and attention. On the other hand, we fully understand and expect that many of you will skim this chapter. You'll make it through much more quickly that way, but you will likely misss some of the finer details. (Did you catch it *that* time?)

Psychologists Keith Rayner and Monica Castelhano have mapped how our eyes move when reading closely versus when we are skimming,[11] as the following image illustrates. The circles indicate where participants' eyes focus and pause; those locations are called "fixations." The lines indicate where the eyes move during the time between fixations. During close reading, the eyes move from word to word in sequence. But when skimming, the eyes have fewer fixations and jump across lines.

Skimming often involves skipping words, phrases, and even paragraphs. It also often involves jumping forward in anticipation, and jumping backward to review or find something initially missed. We take in words out of order, and skip over a lot of them completely. That is why skimming is faster than reading, but also why it leaves us susceptible to missing information.

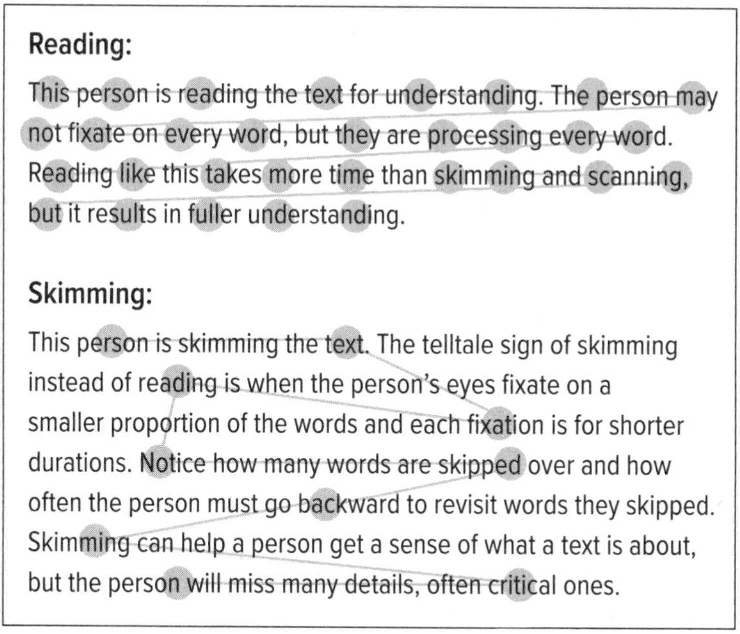

Reading:

This person is reading the text for understanding. The person may not fixate on every word, but they are processing every word. Reading like this takes more time than skimming and scanning, but it results in fuller understanding.

Skimming:

This person is skimming the text. The telltale sign of skimming instead of reading is when the person's eyes fixate on a smaller proportion of the words and each fixation is for shorter durations. Notice how many words are skipped over and how often the person must go backward to revisit words they skipped. Skimming can help a person get a sense of what a text is about, but the person will miss many details, often critical ones.

Keep in mind that skimming is not some kind of cheating. It is an extremely useful strategy for minimizing the amount of time and attention required to extract key information. And people skim all the time, not just when reading long books. In a recent survey that we conducted, participants reported skimming nearly 40% of their emails and 20% of their text messages.[12]

In addition to skimming, busy readers use a complementary time-saving strategy called "scanning." Scanning involves jumping between sections of a text, often guided by our selective attention and rules of thumb about where the most valuable information is likely to be. Readers often expect the first sentence of a paragraph to orient them to what the rest of the paragraph is about. Guided by that expectation, they may spend more time reading those opening sentences and use them to decide what (if anything) to read more closely.[13] Or they may approach the text at a higher level, reading the headings until they find a section they want to examine more closely by either skimming or close reading it.

Researchers can observe this scanning process in action when they track how our eyes wander through reading material.[14] Readers skip over large swaths of text, mainly landing on anchor points: headings, first sentences of paragraphs, images, and formatting that visually contrasts with the rest of the text. Readers then skip all the text under some anchor points yet carefully read the text under others. As with skimming, readers who are scanning sometimes jump backward to revisit sections previously skipped over.

Part of being an effective writer is helping readers manage time efficiently. If the point of your message is simply the

☑ **Tip: The rubber impeller is located inside a stainless steel cup and uses the water for lubrication. If this water is not present, the friction of the rubber on stainless steel will very rapidly overheat and destroy the rubber impeller. This is why it's imperative NOT to operate, or even turn over, your outboard without there being a proper supply of water to the outboard beforehand.**

As a general rule, inspect the impeller and water pump assembly every year if operating in salt, brackish, or turbid water, and replace if necessary. The debris in these waters acts like sandpaper. If operating in freshwater that is clear and clean, this interval may likely stretch to two seasons, provided no dry operation has occurred. Be sure to check your particular owner's manual for your outboard's specific service interval.

☑ **Tip: If you're at all uneasy about performing impeller/water pump inspection and replacement procedures, have your local Yamaha Marine dealer do the work. They have the tools, materials, and training to do it right, for your peace of mind.**

Belts and Hoses

Any belts and hoses your outboard has have to operate in the brutally harsh marine environment. Give them a glance once in a while and heed the manufacturer's schedule for their replacement. If you find cracking or fraying, be safe and replace. Do not attempt to "flip" a belt in order to extend its life, nor should you handle the belt with lubricant of any kind on your fingers. Keep these safe from spray-on lubricants, too.

☑ **Tip: Yamaha four-stroke outboard timing belts and HDPI® two-stroke outboard high-pressure fuel pump belts are cogged and Kevlar®-impregnated, making them super-tough and non-stretchable. Still, Yamaha recommends they be changed every five years or every 1,000 hours.**

Spark Plugs

As a general rule, pull four-stroke outboard spark plugs every 200 hours or every other season and check for proper color and wear. They should be a light brownish color and have relatively sharp edges. When necessary, replace with the exact manufacturer and part number that your outboard's manufacturer stipulates. The brand type and style of spark plugs used in your outboard are by design. They contain specific performance attributes that are engineered into your outboard. Those little markings and numbers on your spark plugs contain a wealth of information about heat range, thread depth, etc.—so don't second-guess or try to cross-reference here. Your outboard's performance depends on it.

Air Intake Passages

Be sure to check the air intake passages for any obstructions such as bird nests and other debris brought in by various critters. Look under your cowling, too. It doesn't take long for your outboard or boat to become home to local birds and bugs, and it can be a real headscratcher when it comes to performance-loss diagnosis.

Thermostats and Pop-Off Valves

These are responsible for regulating the operating temperature of your outboard. Simple and effective, they're best observed through any signs of change in the engine's operating temperature. Operating in saltwater can cause deposits to build up, causing the valves to stick open, which can over-cool the outboard and prevent it from reaching proper operating temperature. Small bits of debris in the cooling water can get lodged between mating surfaces and cause the same condition. If this happens, removal and cleaning is most often the [illegible]. Check your owner's manual for specific replacement recommendations.

experience of reading it, you likely want to signal up front that what you have written is worth reading in full. But if, as is more often the case, the point of your message is to convey important information or to request an action, you need to meet the busy readers on their own terms. They are going to skim and scan regardless. Writing in a way that helps them grasp key information as they do so will make their reading flow more smoothly while also helping you accomplish your goals as a writer.

DECIDING WHETHER TO RESPOND

If you have managed to engage successfully with your busy reader, you still have to get past another mental hurdle: the decision about whether and how to respond. Many communications explicitly ask readers to take action, such as completing a form, scheduling a meeting, responding to a question or request, paying a bill, and so on. Regardless of specifics, the likelihood that the reader will perform that action depends heavily on how well the request is communicated and on how easy it is to fulfill. Like all the decisions we make, this calculation is complicated by our busy lives and by our tendency to procrastinate.

There are three main reasons why readers might not follow through on a requested action.

First, the readers might not understand the request being made. This issue comes back to a core part of effective writing. If readers have to put in extra effort to decipher the meaning of a message, they will be much less likely to respond. They may get distracted, postpone trying to make sense of the request, or simply give up and move on. As a result, they may fail to take action in a timely manner, if at all. The effective writer therefore needs to focus on the *clarity* of the message.

Second, the readers might not think the action is important or necessary. Another crucial aspect of your job as an effective writer is making it clear why a message matters, and why it matters to this reader in particular. The effective writer therefore needs to establish the *relevance* of the message.

Finally, even if the readers understand what they're being asked and accept that it is worthwhile to respond, they may delay acting until later—especially if the requested action seems time-consuming to complete. Often we have the best of intentions to follow through, but you know how that goes . . . You can send reminders later, but it is far better to create the conditions for the reader to act now, before procrastination kicks in.

Writers have only so much control over how busy readers engage and respond. For instance, every election year, voter registration efforts in the US spend enormous amounts of time and money trying to convince the public to register to vote. There is little that pamphlet writers can do to simplify the registration process for citizens. What effective writers *can* do is describe and present the process as clearly and simply as possible. In later chapters of the book, we will show you how to do that, step by step.

Before you can start to write for busy readers, though, you must be very clear about *why* you are writing: To communicate effectively, you need to know your goals. Many writers fail to clear this final, major mental hurdle. Fortunately, there are strategies to help you out here, too.

3

Know Your Goals

Effective writing is about transferring key information from the writer to the reader. Getting the busy reader to engage and react is only part of the process. You also have to know, very clearly, what it is you are trying to achieve with your writing. What do you want the reader to understand? How do you want the reader to respond?

For simplicity, you can pose the most essential version of these questions to yourself: If your reader is going to spend just five seconds on your message, *what is the most important information you want them to come away with?* If you don't know your goals as a writer, it's impossible to effectively convey them to readers.

Figuring out your goals can be harder than it seems, in part because writers are busy, too. Many of us fire off emails and text messages while juggling dozens of other things. When we are busy, it's hard to stop and carefully consider what we're trying to say. It is much easier to send off quick thoughts that follow our stream of consciousness. Sometimes when we write an initial draft of a message, we're not even sure what our goals are. Yet, if we don't prioritize our goals for our readers, then readers are left to interpret what's important on their own. And they may come away with a different understanding of what's important than we might have intended.

Fortunately, the writing process itself can help you gain clarity: Honing your skills as an effective writer will also hone your skills as a lucid thinker. Organizational psychologist and best-selling author Adam Grant makes the point clearly: "Turning thoughts into words sharpens reasoning. What's fuzzy in your head is clear on the page."[1]

Most writers are accustomed to checking for the simplest of writing flaws: typos and basic errors such as incorrect words or mangled grammar. Even so, these flaws are astonishingly common. Just think how many of them you have seen recently in official work emails, office memos, school updates, and the like—never mind the ones that show up in more casual text messages or social media posts. Anything that disrupts the flow of words distracts the reader. Typos can also undermine your goals by implicitly telling the reader, "This note is not important enough to edit." Busy readers will happily reciprocate by ignoring the *real* message you intended to send. Taking the time to clean up your words and present them readably is a first step toward engaging your reader.

But effective writing requires taking the revision process quite a bit further than that. Starting with an initial draft, effective writers will revise, and revise again, until we understand our own goals. We did so repeatedly in the course of writing this book. More surprising, perhaps, we routinely revise and rewrite our emails, memos, and even text messages. That behavior might seem like overkill, but the rewards are significant. Once you get into the habit of goal-focused revision, you will notice that your own ideas become clearer, and that the things you write are more likely to achieve the impact you were aiming for.

Not sure how to be an effective rewriter? On each revision, continually ask yourself these two essential questions: "What is the most important information I want my readers to understand?" and "How do I make it easier for my readers to understand it?" Keep in mind that you cannot achieve your goals as a writer if you are unclear on what those goals are! Once you know the answer, you are ready to begin the process of ensuring that your writing accomplishes those goals.

The rest of this book is designed to guide you through that process. We have distilled six principles to help you get your key information (once you know what it is!) through to busy readers. The principles also address a tension that is inherent in all writing: Readers approach text with their own goals, and those goals may not align with writers' goals. We've already discussed why readers might decide to skim or scan or procrastinate—all of these strategies may undermine writers' goals if a message is not written effectively. In the following chapters, we will discuss how effective writers recognize this tension and write accordingly, rather than asking or expecting readers to change their goals and behavior.

Remember that if a reader overlooks information that we consider important and fails to act the way we want, *that is not the reader's fault.* If this happens, we, as writers, have failed.

In his book *The Design of Everyday Things*, Don Norman argues that if a person tries to use a common object, such as a door handle, a light switch, or an oven, and gives up before figuring it out, that is the designer's fault. Norman founded the user-centered design movement and has spent his career studying these issues. His point is that no matter how beautiful or elegant that object might be, the designer's essential job is to meet people where they are by creating objects that are easy to use. We have a similar perspective on practical writing. Our job as writers is to meet busy readers where they are, and as they are.

We bear the burden of writing effectively for our readers. But hopefully that burden won't seem quite so heavy after you are done reading this book.

PART TWO

Six Principles of Effective Writing

4

First Principle: Less Is More

Brevity is the soul of wit," said Polonius in William Shakespeare's *Hamlet*. Shakespeare crafted this sentence with a clever dual meaning. It is ironic: *Hamlet* is his longest play, and Polonius is his most long-winded character. It is also entirely sincere, however. Shakespeare, perhaps more than any other writer, understood the enduring power of a compelling idea told in a brief and memorable way. Many of his turns of phrase have become a standard part of our everyday language, and four hundred years later Polonius's words still stand as sage advice.

And yet there is a distressingly widespread misconception among writers that more is better. Perhaps it stems from memories of being a student and pushing to reach the required word count of a ninth-grade essay. It might reflect the hope that writing a lot will make it seem like we are smart and have a lot to say. Conversely, it might reflect a fear that if we don't write a lot we will leave out some critical piece of information. Whatever the cause of all this verbal excess, the reality is more writing leads readers to be less likely to read anything.

First and foremost, more writing takes more time to read. The average American adult takes in about 240 words per minute when reading nonfiction—just four words per second.[1] Although the time required to read an additional few words or sentences can seem trivial, it quickly adds up. More writing also requires more concentration. Both academic research and our own personal observations confirm that readers are more likely to read messages that include fewer words, ideas, and requests. In fact, modern readers have developed a shorthand expression for how they feel about overwhelmingly verbose writing. "TL;DR" has become a common, sarcastic—and *short*—way to note that something is "too long; [so I] didn't read."

Although concise writing saves time and effort on the part of the reader, it requires more time and effort from the writer. The seventeenth-century mathematician Blaise Pascal captured this trade-off when he apologized that "I would have written a shorter letter if I'd had more time."[2] (The quote has also been attributed to Mark Twain, John Locke, and many others, affirming how widely people relate to the sentiment.) Long-winded writing is relatively simple to execute; we can transcribe our stream of consciousness directly into written words. Translating our unstructured thoughts into clear, concise, and articulate messages involves more serious work.

Most of us have never been trained in the skill of concise writing. Compounding the problem, most of us have not been trained in the skill of concise editing (or self-editing), either. Researchers have found that people tend to add words and content while editing, rather than remove them. In one illustrative study by Gabrielle Adams and colleagues at the University of Virginia, test subjects were asked to read and summarize a short article about the discovery of King Richard III's bones beneath a parking lot in Leicester, England. After completing their summary, they were then asked to edit it and improve how well it captured the ideas in the article. In response, 83% of participants *added* words.[3] The same pattern showed up across topics ranging from travel itineraries to patents: We tend to add ideas rather than subtract or remove them in the editing process.[4]

We think of the additional effort required to write concisely as an investment. Busy readers are more likely to make time to engage with short, clear, well-structured messages. And if they do engage, they are then more likely to take away the most critical information. Spending a little more time up front to be concise can save writers a great deal of time in the end, by reducing follow-ups, misunderstandings, and requests left unfulfilled.

MORE DETERS READERS

"Less is more" is not just a useful motto. It is also a documented truth about the way busy readers behave: Longer messages deter readers from engaging and encourage them to procrastinate. Imagine you open your inbox and you see the following two messages on the next page. From the subject lines and senders, you know that they're work related. You don't engage with the messages other than to quickly scan their lengths.

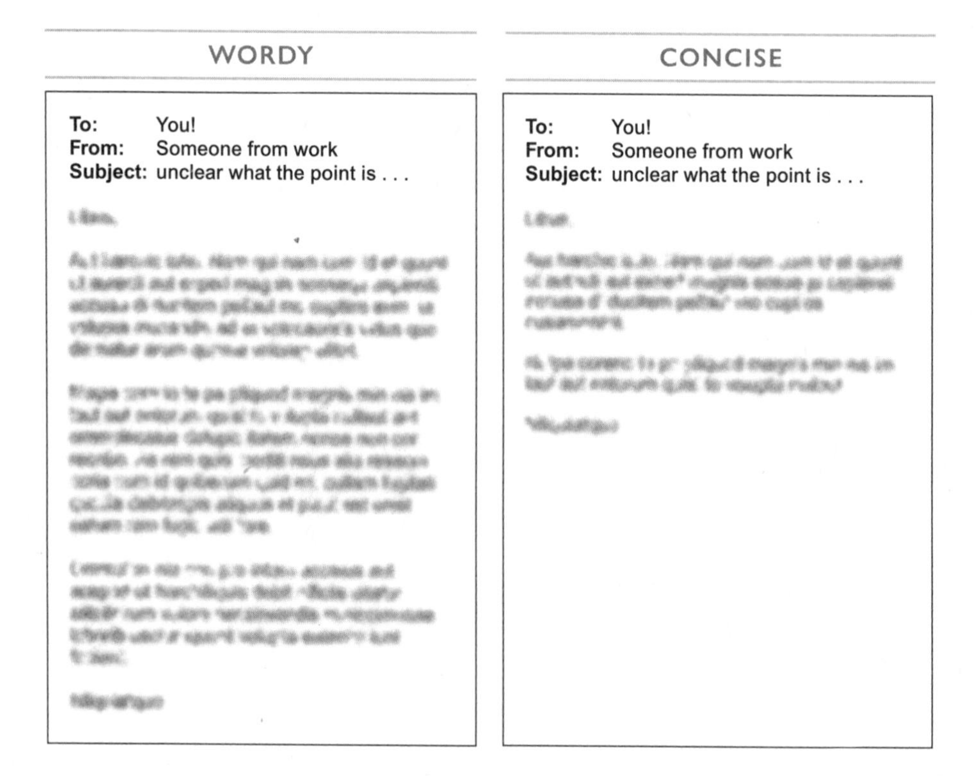

Which would you deal with first? Probably the *Concise* one, right? In a survey we conducted, that's what 165 out of 166 professionals said, too.[5]

Readers often interpret the length of a message as an indication of how difficult and time-consuming it will be to respond to, which is another reason why they might choose not to engage with a wordy communication. In one study, we sent two versions of an email to 7,002 school board members across the US requesting that they complete a short online survey.[6] One email was 127 words; the other was 49 words.

WORDY

Hello,
I am a professor at Harvard studying the opinions, decision-making, goals, and expectations of school board members. As a school board member, you have an important and difficult job. You and your fellow school board members are making critical decisions right now that will profoundly impact the lives of students, teachers, and families in your schools and communities. I know you are busy with many urgent and important decisions as your schools reopen. School district leaders like you are balancing many competing interests. Your participation will be very helpful to the research I am conducting. I would like to learn from you how school-district leaders are thinking about the challenges facing schools right now. Would you please complete this brief survey? The link is here: http://surveylink.com.

Thank you for your time,
Dr. Todd Rogers, Professor of Public Policy

CONCISE

Hello,
I am a professor at Harvard studying the opinions, decision-making, goals, and expectations of school board members. ~~As a school board member, you have an important and difficult job. You and your fellow school board members are making critical decisions right now that will profoundly impact the lives of students, teachers, and families in your schools and communities. I know you are busy with many urgent and important decisions as your schools reopen. School district leaders like you are balancing many competing interests. Your participation will be very helpful to the research I am conducting.~~ I would like to learn from you how school district leaders are thinking about the challenges facing schools right now. Would you please complete this brief survey? The link is here: http://surveylink.com.

Thank you for your time,
Dr. Todd Rogers, Professor of Public Policy

The *Concise* email yielded nearly twice as many survey responses as the *Wordy* email—a 4.8% response rate instead of 2.7%. Some readers likely looked at the length of the *Wordy* email and chose not to engage with it at all. Others likely didn't read all the way through it and missed the request at the end. In addition, some readers may have used the length of the email as a signal of how long it would take to complete the survey and decided to pass on the request (which they presumed would be taxing). Both emails directed recipients to the exact same survey, which took approximately five minutes to complete. Yet, in a separate study, 29% of respondents who saw the *Concise* email believed the survey would take less than five minutes, compared to just 15% of respondents who saw the *Wordy* email. Most readers, but especially those who are pressed for time, are likely to be put off by messages and requests that they expect will be difficult to deal with.[7]

Readers who drop out in the middle of a long message engage in what we call "early quitting." They may skim the text and decide it is too much to deal with at that moment—too many topics, requested actions, or words—and move on before finishing, hoping to return to it later. Some of these early quitters will never actually return. Others may come back to the message later, but by then they may have missed a critical moment: A payment deadline may have passed, an insurance enrollment window may have closed, or all the available meeting times may have been filled.

On average, a wordy message will be dealt with less quickly than a concise message. In the worst case, a wordy message will be relegated to the same fate as the hundreds of other messages that languish in inboxes, never to be read. The inverse of the motto is perhaps even more relevant here: *More is less.*

MORE DILUTES INFORMATION

Messages containing more words, ideas, or requests also tend to dilute each individual piece of information they contain. When messages include more content, readers are less likely to notice, understand, or act upon the most critical content, for two reasons.

First, readers who are skimming may conclude that they've understood the gist of the message and move on when, in fact, they missed the writer's main point. If a message includes only a few sentences and a single idea, even a quick skim is likely to reveal the central idea. But with longer messages, readers may inadvertently skip over important content without realizing it. They may also search for specific content or ideas they're interested in and move on once they have found it—whether that content is the thing that mattered most to the writer. In other words, the readers might satisfy their own goals while leaving the writer's goals unmet.

Second, longer messages are more likely to deplete readers' attention and focus. In a study with the wonderful title "TL;DR: Longer Sections of Text Increase Rates of Unintentional Mind-Wandering," a group of American and Canadian researchers reported that readers' attention is more likely to drift when reading longer messages.[8] Readers who get distracted and don't make it through the entire wordy message may then miss the writer's key information.

Writing concisely requires a ruthless willingness to cut unnecessary words, sentences, paragraphs, and ideas. It can be hard to delete the words that you spent time crafting—to "murder your darlings," as advised in the classic lectures compiled in *On the Art of Writing*.[9] But doing so increases the chances that your audience will read what you write. Nancy Gibbs, former editor in chief of *Time* magazine, would tell her staff that every word has to earn its place in a sentence, every sentence has to earn its place in a paragraph, and every idea has to earn its place in a text.[10]

THE LIMITS OF LESS

Although concise messages demonstrably outperform wordy messages, most people wrongly predict that wordier messages will be more effective.[11] This contradiction is driven, in part, by a fundamental tension in many types of common writing. We want to communicate with the reader precisely but also completely. We want the reader to engage and react, but we also want the reader to be aware of us as a writer with nuance, emotion, and style.

It is possible to balance these contradictions, but at a cost.

Sometimes you may find that it is worth the cost of saying more. For instance, we conducted an experiment with a school district during the Covid pandemic, while they were teaching remotely. We showed them that a concise message yielded more parent responses than a wordy message (we will talk more on this later in the chapter). The school district decided to continue using the wordy message anyway.

Why would a school district intentionally send a "less effective" message to parents? Because, in this case, doing so helped them accomplish a more important purpose than getting responses to a school survey. Their paramount goal was rebuilding warm relationships with parents after a tumultuous year of remote schooling. Getting parents to complete the survey was a secondary goal. After weighing these priorities, the school district decided that the longer message came across as more emotional and human. It did more to serve their overall goals, even if it yielded fewer survey responses.

The bottom line is that effective writing needs to be appropriate to the context of the communication. We can provide the guidelines, but you have to make the informed decisions about how to balance your desire to include more words, ideas, and requests with the many constraints facing a busy reader. We do *not* recommend that writers categorically use the shortest possible messages. Rather, we recommend cutting all that can be cut, and no more, to suit your goals. Different contexts may require different considerations. But more often than people think, less is more when it comes to writing for busy people.

Now let's look at how to put "less is more" to work in your effective writing.

THE RULES OF "LESS IS MORE"

Rule 1: Use Fewer Words

"Omit needless words" is one of the enduring messages of Strunk and White's *Elements of Style*, and is an easy first step toward more concise writing.[12] "Whether" is better than "whether or not." "In spite of the fact that" can be replaced with "though." "Because" can easily take the place of "for the reason that." Replacements like these (and the others listed in the table on the next page) have nearly identical meanings but use fewer words, making messages visually shorter and requiring less time to read. The appendix includes a more extensive list.

Replace this . . . ***(Wordy)***	**. . . with this** ***(Concise)***
costs the sum of	costs
for the reason that	because
in the near future	soon
that being the case	if so
whether or not	whether
personal opinion	opinion
he is a man who	he
there is no doubt that	clearly
ask the question	ask
had done previously	had done
hurry up	hurry
off of	off
plunge down	plunge
soft to the touch	soft
spell out in detail	spell out
start off	start
with the exception of	except
described as	called
in order to	to
one of the reasons	one reason

Omitting truly *needless* words makes your writing shorter without sacrificing meaning or precision. Getting rid of long-winded phrases is therefore relatively uncontroversial. But sometimes effective writing calls for sacrificing words that are not quite needless, even if they are not quite crucial, either. Sometimes it is worth losing a little precision and meaning to save readers' time.

A study we conducted with an organization called the Journalist's Resource illustrates the benefits of strategic omission. The organization sends weekly emails that include resources on timely topics for journalists; those emails go out to more than fifty thousand recipients. In August 2020, the professional writers at the organization wrote a newsletter offering subscribers six resources to learn more about wage theft by employers. At our suggestion, they edited their original newsletter to create a more concise version containing half as many words (275 instead of the original 566) but preserving all six linked resources.

The concise version of the Journalist's Resource newsletter retained the key content they wanted to share, such as a study showing that wage theft is more likely when companies are performing poorly. But to reduce the word count, the edited newsletter omitted lower-priority supporting details, such as a quote from the author that the writers considered relevant but not necessary. Half of the newsletter subscribers received the original version; the other half received the concise version. The concise version led to twice as many subscribers clicking on the resource links as the original.[13] Removing the less important details lost a little bit of information but substantially *increased* readers' engagement with the message.

A separate study analyzing communications within a consulting firm reached the same conclusion. Researchers found that employees responded more quickly to shorter, more focused emails than to longer ones. When the researchers presented these results to a group of executives at the firm, they showed two actual emails—one focused and one rambling—and asked the executives themselves how they would handle the long, rambling message. More than one executive responded, "I'd delete it."[14]

Rule 2: Include Fewer Ideas

Concise writing is not just about limiting the total word count. It is also about limiting the number of distinct ideas in a message. Imagine if you received the following text from a friend:

> **I'm looking forward to our 6:30 dinner tonight. Let's eat at Tina's Italian Restaurant at 651 Ocean Drive. Their breadsticks are awesome, I had them this past spring. I haven't had their lasagna, but I'm ready. It's supposed to be tasty. Let's meet at my place 15 minutes early and we'll walk from there. Sam and Joey are going to join us for dinner too.**

Notice that this message contains at least eight ideas:

- The writer is looking forward to the dinner at 6:30
- The dinner location will be Tina's Italian Restaurant
- Tina's Italian Restaurant's address is 651 Ocean Drive
- Tina's Italian Restaurant has good breadsticks, which the writer tried in the spring
- The writer has not had Tina's Italian Restaurant's lasagna

- The writer heard that Tina's Italian Restaurant's lasagna is tasty
- The writer wants the reader to come to the writer's place at 6:15
- Sam and Joey are joining the dinner

That's a lot of information! It's an extreme case, but it illustrates the kind of excess that we have all experienced. A lot of us are guilty of creating that kind of excess, too.

The writer of the message seemingly wants the reader to know all eight ideas, but from context it seems that the most important idea is the seventh one: the meeting time and location. Including all the other ideas decreases the chance that the reader holds on to that one key idea. The reader may be deterred by the sheer number of words and ideas and decide not to engage at all. Or they may read the whole message but be distracted by the other seven ideas and not remember or focus on the information that was most critical to the writer. Either way, cutting the number of ideas can help ensure readers take away the most important point. The entire text could be condensed to: *Dinner is on. Meet at my place at 6:15.*

Like cutting words, cutting ideas often requires discarding less important but still relevant information to emphasize the more important information. This can greatly improve clarity even in brief forms of communication like text messaging. As a test, we texted a request to complete a one-minute online survey to parents in a large public school district at the beginning of the Covid pandemic. Half of the 22,694 parents received a thirty-six-word text, which we'll call the *Wordy* message (even though thirty-six words is hardly verbose). The other half received a twenty-word version, which we'll call the *Concise* message.

WORDY

TEXT MESSAGE 1: Thank you for participating in [district] summer updates! We know distance learning can be hard. We want to help and to hear from you.

TEXT MESSAGE 2: Please answer this 1-minute survey to help us improve our program:

[survey link]

CONCISE

TEXT MESSAGE 1: Thank you for participating in [district] summer updates!

TEXT MESSAGE 2: Please answer this 1-minute survey to help us improve our program:

[survey link]

The *Wordy* message included two sentences intended to acknowledge and empathize with the struggles parents were experiencing at that stage of the pandemic. Those sentences may have added warmth, but they also introduced a separate idea from the request to participate in the survey. The *Concise* text message ended up yielding 6% more parent responses than the *Wordy* one, a small but meaningful difference.

In another experiment, we measured the impact of using fewer ideas and fewer words in a fundraising email that was sent to 776,145 potential donors to a political candidate for statewide office. The campaign's original *Wordy* version contained six paragraphs, culminating in a donation appeal. It included several compelling facts, including the latest poll numbers and an update on the opponent's fundraising progress. Conventional wisdom in the fundraising world is that longer messages are more effective, so we were curious to put that notion to the test.

When we reviewed the *Wordy* version, we couldn't decide which ideas were the most important, other than the essential request to donate. With the campaign's permission, we created a *Concise* version by arbitrarily deleting every other paragraph, cutting the number of ideas roughly in half. The majority of an independent sample of respondents found the *Concise* email to flow less coherently from one paragraph to the next compared to the *Wordy* one.[15] Nevertheless, when the campaign tested the two messages against each other, the *Concise* version raised 16% more money than the *Wordy* original.

WORDY

To: You!
From: [CANDIDATE NAME]
Date: [DATE]
Subject: [SUBJECT LINE]

I wanted you to hear this incredible news from me first, [YOUR NAME]:

Poll after poll has shown me running neck and neck with unelected [OPPOSING CANDIDATE NAME](R) in the race that [REDACTED].

Now, our people-powered campaign is officially surging—a brand-new FiveThirtyEight polling analysis shows us [POINTS] ahead, [X% to X%]!

But here's the bad news: Republicans are now scrambling. On top of the [$] million [OPPOSING CANDIDATE NAME] is already spending to buy this seat, Mitch McConnell and his shady GOP allies just pledged to pour in another [$] MILLION to crush our momentum and hold on to their extremist majority.

Republicans know that if we lose in [STATE], Democrats will [REDACTED]. Plain and simple. **That's why we set a goal to raise $25,000 by midnight tonight to keep up our momentum, fight back against GOP attacks and win this race.**

But right now, we're coming up incredibly short. If we don't close this gap, [OPPOSING CANDIDATE NAME] could retake the lead—and [REDACTED]. So I have to ask:

Please, [YOUR NAME], will you rush a gift of $[X] or more now to help us hit our grassroots goal, flip [STATE] blue and [REDACTED]?

Thanks so much for pitching in what you can.

[CANDIDATE NAME]

CONCISE

To: You!
From: [CANDIDATE NAME]
Date: [DATE]
Subject: [SUBJECT LINE]

I wanted you to hear this incredible news from me first, [YOUR NAME]:

Now, our people-powered campaign is officially surging—a brand-new FiveThirtyEight polling analysis shows us [POINTS] ahead, [X% to X%]!

Republicans know that if we lose in [STATE], Democrats will [REDACTED]. Plain and simple. **That's why we set a goal to raise $25,000 by midnight tonight to keep up our momentum, fight back against GOP attacks and win this race.**

Please, [YOUR NAME], will you rush a gift of $[X] or more now to help us hit our grassroots goal, flip [STATE] blue and [REDACTED]?

Thanks so much for pitching in what you can.

[CANDIDATE NAME]

One way or another, almost all writers will face a trade-off between reaching more readers using fewer ideas or fewer readers using more ideas. There are no universal rules for how many ideas are too many or for which ideas are important to keep, but there is the same standby principle: Cut as much as possible within your specific context. As with words, more ideas can both deter readers from engaging and decrease the chance that readers will grasp key information if they do engage.

Rule 3: Make Fewer Requests

Deleting the precious words and ideas we've written can be difficult, but effective practical writing requires a third type of self-restraint that can be the most challenging of all: asking for less. Often we want readers to take multiple actions, such as reviewing documents, replying to questions, supplying information, or even reconsidering core beliefs about, say, immigration or the environment. Before you start loading up on your goals, remember how easily readers get derailed and distracted and how they struggle with multitasking. Asking busy readers for *more* can cause them to do *less*.

Imagine receiving a message from a colleague containing two requests: that you review a long document, and that you respond to a question you already know the answer to. The former is relatively time-consuming. The latter might take you just a couple minutes. You might postpone doing either task until you have time to do both. Or, if you have time, you may begin one of them. Since we tend to start with things we expect to be easier, you'll probably answer the question first. But then you might move on to the next task in your queue and forget about the harder request, reviewing the long document.

Experiences like this happen to us often. They can have far-reaching consequences, especially when the request relates to an important issue. With that in mind, a group of researchers recently set out to learn what messages most effectively mobilize people to take actions to mitigate climate change.[16] The researchers informed a set of more than 1,500 participants about the dangers of climate change and asked them to take action. They then provided some of the readers with a list of twenty relatively easy actions they could take to reduce their personal environmental impact, such as turning off lights and appliances and purchasing a low-flow showerhead. They provided other readers with just one, five, or ten suggested actions.

Offering fewer suggestions (one, five, or ten options) led to an average of two more actions being taken than offering twenty relatively easy suggestions. It's possible that participants who were provided with twenty suggested actions found the message overwhelming and couldn't decide which ones to perform. It's also possible the largest number of suggested actions simply deterred some from reading them at all. We don't know the exact cognitive mechanism at work, but we do know that readers who were given more options were less likely to do any of them.

Not only can overloading readers with requests decrease the likelihood that they will take action, it can also decrease the likelihood that the readers notice and remember key information in the message. For instance, if the participants who were provided with twenty suggested environmentally friendly actions were deterred from reading the message entirely, they would have missed other important information about climate change, separate from the list of actions.

The need to make fewer requests of readers again puts pressure on writers to prioritize their goals. The popular website *Behavioral Scientist* implemented a program to increase sales of their print magazine. They sent a set of their subscribers a promotional email containing information about the current print edition of their magazine along with a link to learn more, as well as similar information and a link for the most recent past issue. The magazine team's top priority was promoting the latest issue, but they figured that as long as they had people's attention they might as well promote the previous issue, too.

Since *Behavioral Scientist* is run by (you guessed it) behavioral scientists, they decided to test whether removing the lower-priority request from the email would increase engagement with their higher-priority request: getting readers to click on the link to learn more about the current issue. Presenting just a single link in the email resulted in 50% more clicks on that link. Putting in a second link may have seemed like a "bonus" that would drive more reader engagement, but it had the opposite effect. Including a second link, to the past issue, diverted readers from the most important request, sharply reducing the likelihood that they performed it at all.

Another study shows the same pattern among the readers of an email newsletter. The National Bureau of Economic Research is a network of leading economic scholars that produces a highly regarded weekly newsletter about new work in that field. Each newsletter contains a brief description of all journal articles submitted that week by the organization's members, along with a link to each of those articles. The number of articles included each week varies widely; one week it might include ten papers, but the next week it might include thirty.

Researchers at the bureau ran a study to see whether adding more papers to their weekly newsletter affected the impact each paper had on the field and the amount of coverage it got in the media.[17] Consistent with the "less is more" theme, they found that when newsletters included more papers, readers clicked on each individual paper less frequently. On average, doubling the number of papers in a given week decreased any specific paper's media coverage by 30%. It also decreased, though to a less dramatic extent, how many times readers clicked on the link to view the scholarly paper, how many times they downloaded the paper, and how many times the paper was cited by other scholars.

Like all of us, readers of the economics newsletter have a limited amount of time and attention. When faced with more demands for attention—a larger number of papers to click on—they didn't devote more time to the task. They simply clicked less on each one. Apparently, the impact of future Nobel Prize–worthy research will depend, in part, on whether it is released during a slow news week.

We see the same effect play out (though on a smaller scale) in our daily lives: We text a friend with two questions and get a reply to only one. We receive a work email noting multiple tasks and we follow through on only one of them, or none at all. Simply put: Brevity matters.

5

Second Principle: Make Reading Easy

There's an episode of the TV series *Seinfeld* in which the show's protagonist, Jerry Seinfeld, gets into an accident in a rental car. When he returns the damaged car, he's surprised to learn that the insurance policy he purchased won't cover the damage. As he's arguing with the rental car agent, she begins to chide him, "Sir, if you had read the rental agreement—" Seinfeld interrupts, using his trademark indignant voice, "Did you see the size of that document? It's like the Declaration of Independence, who's gonna read that?"

Seinfeld's retort touches on two major impediments to effective practical writing: length and complexity. We've already seen that the length of a written message can deter readers from engaging and make them less likely to grasp the key information in it if they do. Complexity can cause similar problems by making the reading process overly difficult and tiresome.

"Readability" is a way to judge how complex a message is; it provides a quantifiable measure of how easy or difficult it is to read. There are multiple formulas for measuring readability, but it is typically determined by analyzing the types of words used, the lengths of the sentences, and the overall structure and syntax of the writing. The resulting assessments help in teaching people to read, in matching students with appropriately challenging texts, and in evaluating a reader's capability. The United States military led the first efforts to develop readability metrics in 1917, just as the country was entering World War I, to evaluate whether soldiers could read well enough to perform their jobs.[1]

Readability measures are usually presented as either a numerical score or the school grade a reader would need to complete to understand the text, based on the US education system. For instance, a text written at a seventh-grade reading level should be comprehensible to the average seventh-grade student. Understanding *The New York Times* requires reading at an eleventh-grade reading level; understanding typical nursery rhymes requires reading at a fourth-grade level.

There are some obvious issues with the grade-level measurement, since school systems and standards vary dramatically around the US (not to mention the rest of the world). But for effective writers, the key concept is the nature of readability itself. Shorter and more common words are inherently easier to read, as are shorter and simpler sentences.

READABLE WRITING IS EFFECTIVE

"I don't need much to stop reading a document. So if I don't understand it, I won't read it."

"It was all in the English language, yet I could not understand the mumbo jumbo!! This for me feels condescending and corrupt."

"I wondered: Why should I have to do the work?"[2]

We can all relate to these quotes from nonlawyers describing their experience of working with lawyers. Every field has its own specialized terms and jargon, but lawyers seem to take it to an art form. Complex, difficult-to-read messages are less likely to be read; if they *are* read, they're less likely to be understood. Yet, too often practical communications are written without an eye toward readability. Anyone who has signed a contract, a lease, or (like Jerry Seinfeld) a rental car agreement is familiar with the barrage of impenetrable, ineffective legal mumbo jumbo.

Companies know that their terms and conditions and legal documents are rarely read, and have occasionally used this impenetrability to slip in quiet jokes. In 2017, twenty-two thousand people in England unknowingly agreed to one thousand hours of community service while they were signing up for free public wi-fi. The British wi-fi company Purple said that it inserted the clause to demonstrate "the lack of consumer awareness of what they are signing up for."[3] Another company, GameStation, added an April Fool's Day clause to its license agreement in 2010. Unless users took extra steps, GameStation was granted "a non transferable option to claim, for now and for ever more, your immortal soul."[4] We were not able to determine how many souls GameStation has claimed through this agreement.

But the poor readability of everyday writing can have consequences on our mortal lives that are not funny at all. Studies show that up to 60% of patients who sign informed consent forms in healthcare research do not understand the information the forms contain.[5] Is it ethical to enroll participants in a health study that they don't fully understand? Most people would probably say no. On the other hand, important medical advances rely on patients consenting to participate, and the rules of consent are dictated by rules and regulations that are themselves highly complex. Even if the science is hard to explain, we must find better ways to do it.

Is medicine really just too complicated to convey simply? We don't think so. Simplifying writing is possible and doing so can dramatically improve practical communications in most contexts. Increasing readability can improve comprehension of legal documents[6] and textbooks[7] without affecting the core information they communicate.

Even on social media, people engage more with simply written social posts as opposed to complex ones. One study analyzed over four thousand Facebook posts uploaded over a three-year period on *Humans of New York*, a popular photography blog.[8] Simply written posts systematically received more likes, comments, and shares on social media. Increasing the readability by one grade level (i.e., moving from being appropriate for a fifth grader to being appropriate for a fourth grader) was associated with those posts receiving more than sixteen thousand additional likes.

Similar patterns hold true for the ubiquitous online reviews of tourist destinations.[9] Travelers often rely on such reviews to decide where to visit, eat, and sleep, but as the number (and type) of reviews has grown it has become increasingly difficult to assess which reviews to trust. Tripadvisor, the popular travel website, designed a feature called "Was this review helpful?" so that travelers can rate other travelers' reviews. Reviews that score the most votes rise to the top on the site. Researchers analyzed the readability of 41,061 reviews for 106 attractions in New Orleans, Louisiana. No surprise: The more readable a review, the more "helpful" votes it received.

Although increased readability typically translates into increased effectiveness, there are exceptions. In many contexts, readers have strong social or cultural expectations about the style of writing that is appropriate; if the way we write does not match up with those expectations, that can affect how our readers receive the message. For instance, grant proposals submitted to the US National Institutes of Health receive more funding, on average, when the writing is more complex. The same effect has been observed for appeals at fundraising websites like Kickstarter and GoFundMe.[10] In these contexts, readers may associate complex writing with greater effort, intelligence, and seriousness.

That said, at some point, your reader simply will not understand what you are trying to say. You will rarely go wrong with a modified version of "less is more": Aim for the least amount of complexity that will allow you to engage your intended reader. You need to pay attention to context, but remember that more readable writing is fundamentally more effective writing.

READABLE WRITING IS CLEAR

It's important to recognize that writing fewer words does not necessarily make writing easier to understand. After all, one can formulate succinct linguistic units utilizing atypical and immoderate verbiage. (Translation: You can write short sentences using unfamiliar and long words.) It also matters which words you choose. Given two messages with the same number of words, it takes less time and effort to read the one that is written using simpler words.[11]

All else being equal, written communications that are hard to read are both less likely to be engaged with and less likely to be understood if they're engaged with. Readers are more likely to get distracted and mind-wander when reading more complex texts.[12] Readers may even give up and move on if they don't understand a message or don't have the time to devote to understanding it. Writing in an unnecessarily complicated style can have serious real-world consequences: The readability of public texts affects whether patients understand the medical studies they consent to participate in,[13] whether citizens cast votes,[14] and whether parents send their children to school.[15]

Less readable writing also disproportionately affects individuals who have limited English-language literacy, many of whom are members of historically and systemically excluded populations. Around half of American adults read at an eighth-grade level or below.[16] Twenty percent of US adults speak (and read) English as a second language,[17] and some researchers estimate that a similar fraction are affected by dyslexia.[18] For these populations, as well as many others, less readable writing presents an additional barrier to accessibility.

But even the most literate and fluent readers are more likely to read and understand simpler messages than more complex ones. Try the test yourself: Which of the following passages do you find easier to read? If you are like most people, you'll find that you read the eighth-grade-level passage much more quickly and easily.

COLLEGE SOPHOMORE READING LEVEL

Readability measures are represented as single quantitative scores, or as the academic grade level a reader would have needed to complete to be expected to comprehend the text (based on the US system).

For example, The New York Times *is written at an eleventh-grade reading level, while most nursery rhymes are written at a fourth-grade reading level. Using short and familiar words, short sentences, simple sentence structure, and active voice can improve understanding by lowering the required reading level.*

EIGHTH-GRADE READING LEVEL

The readability of text is often shown as a number. Other times it is shown as the academic grade a reader would need to complete to understand the text (based on the US system).

For example, understanding The New York Times *requires an eleventh-grade reading level. Understanding most nursery rhymes requires a fourth-grade reading level. To lower the reading level, use short and familiar words, short sentences, simple tense, and active voice. Doing this can help more readers understand the message.*

Uncle Sam gets this. Federal agencies in the United States are required by law to communicate to the public in a way that is readable. The Plain Writing Act of 2010 requires those agencies to write in "plain" language that members of the public can "understand and use." This rule means every US federal document, from federal tax forms to applications for social security benefits, must be written in clear, simple language. Ironically, the "Federal Plain Language Guidelines"[19] is a 118-page document, written at a tenth-grade reading level. There is a limit to how well the government can regulate effective writing.

Just as writers tend to use too many words and incorporate too many ideas, they also tend toward too much complexity in their language. This problem shows up everywhere, not just in government documents and medical consent forms. In 2019, a pair of legal and business researchers analyzed the terms and conditions agreements from more than five hundred common websites and found that, on average, their readability was comparable to that of scholarly journal articles. At that level, the agreements are inaccessible for the vast majority of adults.[20]

The same is true for credit card agreements, research consent forms, and insurance documents.[21] In some cases, this may be intentional, albeit unethical. Credit card companies may not want customers to read all the terms and conditions so they don't realize the full consequences of racking up late fees and interest for missing payments. Rental car companies may genuinely expect that many customers won't notice the kinds of damage they are liable for. For ill-intentioned corporations or individuals, decreasing the readability of a text is a way to hide information they don't want consumers to know.

Since you are reading this book, we assume you, like us, operate on the other side. We are in the business of trying to ensure that our readers understand what we have to say, so we focus on strategies for improving readability. And we have rules for that, too: The crucial ones are using shorter and more common words and writing straightforward and shorter sentences.[22]

THE RULES OF READABLE WRITING

Rule 1: Use Short and Common Words

More than a century ago, Mark Twain pithily captured the importance of simple language when he said, "Don't use a five-dollar word when a fifty-cent word will do."[23] (Well, *maybe* he said it. The actual origin of the quote is obscure—largely because so many people have related to it and repeated it over the years.) Five-dollar words tend to be more obscure, more complicated, and considered "fancier" than fifty-cent words. What's most important for our purposes is that they also tend to be harder and more time-consuming to read. Think about *acquiesce* versus *agree*: Which is easier to read and understand?

In general, words with fewer syllables and words that are more commonly used can be read more easily and quickly. Google has a tool called the Ngram Viewer that shows how often different English words have been used across all text available online over time.[24] This tool shows that when two words are synonyms, the shorter one generally becomes the more widely written one. *Next* is more common than *subsequent*, *get* is more common than *acquire*, *show* is more common than *demonstrate*, and so on. This is a key element of writing readably: Effective writers let go of their five-dollar pretensions and substitute shorter, more common words for longer, less common ones.

Note that we are merging two concepts here. Shorter words are generally more readable than longer words *and* common words are generally more readable than uncommon words. Very often these concepts converge: For example, the word *slow* has fewer letters and syllables than the word *hinder*, and *slow* is also the more common one. Occasionally, though, length and commonness do not line up. The word *erudite* has fewer syllables than the word *knowledgeable*, but *knowledgeable* is five times as common. In this case, we would lean toward selecting the more common word since more readers will know what it means, even if it is longer.

Your word choices have a cumulative impact, steadily making your writing easier or harder to read. Consider the following two sentences.

Less Readable: *When scribes use sophisticated and unconventional words, it may hinder readers' comprehension.*
More Readable: *When writers use fancy and unusual words, it may slow readers' understanding.*

The two sentences contain the same number of total words (twelve), but the words in the *Less Readable* version have more syllables (twenty-five) than those in the *More Readable* one (twenty-one). The *Less Readable* words are also much less common: "scribes" is less common than "writers," "unconventional" is less common than "unusual," and "hinder" is less common than "slow." Readers may take longer to recognize the less commonly used word, which can slow their reading and tax their attention.

For a real-life example, take this sign posted by a Canadian city that won the WTF Award in 2014 from the Center for Plain Language.[25] (You may associate "WTF" with another meaning, but in this case it stands for "Work That Failed.") Every year, the WTF Award is bestowed on a government communication that is unnecessarily difficult to read.

PERSONS
SHALL
REMOVE ALL
EXCREMENT
FROM PETS
PURSUANT

BY LAW #122-87
MAX. PENALTY
$2000.00

THANK YOU

Who knows how many people failed to pick up after their pets because of this unnecessarily complicated sign. Clearly, it would take even a practiced reader of bureaucratic writing longer to understand this message than it would a message that used shorter and more common words. When we showed this sign to our students, one proposed the message on the next page instead. Seems like a dramatic improvement to us.

Using shorter and more common words can make all types of writing more effective—even tweets, which are already forced to be concise by the rules of the medium (no more than 280 characters allowed per tweet). Researchers analyzed the readability of hundreds of thousands of tweets, based on how common their words were. Tweets using the most common words received about 75% more retweets than tweets using the least common words.[26] So you probably don't want to be tweeting about "pursuant" instructions, either.

Sometimes writers will need to bend the rules of readability to convey a specific message or tone, however. For instance, they might use less common or more complicated words to signal their expertise, intelligence, or importance. Some professional fields have developed specialized vocabularies for talking precisely about concepts that nonspecialists don't need to talk about. In other contexts, writing complexity may be used as a rule of thumb for assessing the competence and intelligence of the writer. This can be particularly consequential in cases where there is a power dynamic between the reader and the writer. Writers who are relatively low-status (for example, in terms of professional rank or social status) may risk being seen as less intelligent if they write simply, whereas higher-status writers may get applauded for being plainspoken.

The problem comes when writers use fancy words unwittingly, in ways that hinder the reader's understanding and the writer's own goals. In many contexts, using words like "sophisticated" instead of "fancy" can come across as pretentious or exclusionary. In an early draft of this book, we used the term "heuristic" instead of "rule of thumb" to describe the conceptual shortcuts people use to reduce the mental effort needed to make decisions or understand situations. The two terms mean the same thing. We initially wrote "heuristic" because it is the standard term used in academia—but it is used hardly anywhere else. We went back, revised, and realized that "rule of thumb" is more effective for our purposes.

The majority of practical writing does not require, or even benefit from, using longer or less common words. And the disadvantages of more complex, less readable language can be significant. In one study, researchers asked participants to read the published ethics codes of 188 publicly traded companies and rate how moral and trustworthy they believed the companies to be. Corporations with less readable ethics codes were rated as less moral and less trustworthy.[27]

Some research suggests that writers who use simpler words actually appear *more* intelligent than those who use less simple ones. The scholarly paper reporting this finding was amusingly titled "Consequences of Erudite Vernacular Utilized Irrespective of Necessity: Problems with Using Long Words Needlessly."[28] It showed that college students rated writers who used complex language to be less intelligent than writers who used simpler language. This paper won the 2006 Ig Nobel Prize for Literature, a prize given to "honor achievements that first make people laugh, and then make them think."

Even in academia there has been a shift toward more readable writing. The association for marketing professionals and scholars, the American Marketing Association, instructs would-be authors that its journal "is designed to be read, not deciphered."[29] The prestigious journal *Nature* specifies that submitted articles should be "written clearly and simply so that they are accessible to readers in other disciplines and to readers for whom English is not their first language."[30] It turns out that academics appreciate effective writing, just like everyone else. One study even found that the most readable scholarly articles are five times as likely to win awards as are the least readable ones.[31]

When you are balancing the trade-offs between readability and using longer, less common but (potentially) more precise words, ask yourself two questions. First, how valuable are the subtle differences in word meaning for conveying the essence of the sentence? Second, is the additional meaning conveyed by the harder-to-read word worth the costs of fewer readers engaging and understanding it and the increased effort required by those who do? Different contexts will call for different solutions, but writers should always weigh the costs they impose on their busy readers. Those five-dollar words may not be worth the cost.

Rule 2: Write Straightforward Sentences

Just as some words take more time and effort to read than others, the same is true of sentences. Humans evolved to speak and listen, long before we developed the ability to read and write. Because we tend to converse in incomplete, short sentences, our brains evolved to make these types of linguistic structures easy to understand. Long, complete sentences are relatively unusual in spoken language, so they challenge our limited mental abilities. This evolutionary perspective can help guide effective writing. It may sound like simple, even childish, advice, but understanding exactly how to write shorter and more straightforward sentences is an extremely useful skill.

There are many grammatical approaches that can improve the readability of sentences, such as using active voice, first person, and parallel structure, and keeping the subject, verb, and object near each other.[32] But these kinds of rules can be complicated to describe, remember, and follow. (How many people know what "parallel sentence structure" means?) For simplicity, we bundle all these approaches into a single guiding concept: *Write so that readers can understand the meaning of a sentence after a single read-through.*

Straightforward sentences proceed in a logical order, with all relevant words and phrases close to each other. Each word builds on the previous one to help readers make sense of the sentence as they work toward its end. This structure allows readers to understand the gist of a sentence quickly and with minimum effort.

Less Straightforward: *The way this sentence is written, given its extra clause and strange phrasing, I wonder if people will understand it.*

More Straightforward: *I wonder if people will understand the way this sentence is written, given its extra clause and strange phrasing.*

Both sentences are grammatically correct and contain the exact same words and phrases. The only difference is that they are ordered differently—but what a difference. The phrase "I wonder if people will understand" relates to "the way this sentence is written." In the *Less Straightforward* version, the phrase "given its extra clause and strange phrasing" interrupts these two components. By the time readers get to "I wonder if people will understand," they may be unsure what phrase it refers to. They may then need to jump back to the beginning of the sentence and try again. Meanwhile, readers of the *More Straightforward* version can make sense of the sentence incrementally as it builds one word and phrase to the next.

Straightforward sentences order relevant words and phrases next to each other, such that they readily make sense after the previous words and phrases. That is, a straightforward sentence doesn't require readers to jump around. Keeping things tight and orderly increases the likelihood readers will understand the full meaning of the sentence in just one pass, decreasing the chance they quit reading altogether.

Rule 3: Write Shorter Sentences

We've already seen the benefits of using fewer words. But even if we hold the total number of words constant, writing shorter sentences usually makes a message easier to read. You can verify this for yourself: It's generally easier to read two ten-word sentences than one twenty-word sentence. That may be one reason why the average length of written sentences has decreased over the years.[33] Novels published in 1800 averaged twenty-seven words per sentence, whereas those published in 2000 averaged just ten words per sentence.[34] In case you were wondering, the decrease in sentence length doesn't mean we have become less intelligent. On the contrary, numerous studies have found rising IQ scores around the globe, a phenomenon known as the Flynn effect.[35]

Inaugural addresses delivered by US presidents have similarly incorporated shorter sentences over time. The first five sentences of President George Washington's address in 1789 averaged sixty-four words, whereas the first five sentences of President Joseph Biden's in 2021 averaged a mere seven words. We're not cherry-picking the data. Nearly everywhere we look, we see a gradual but consistent decline in sentence length.[36]

Scholars debate the reasons for this change, but one of the consequences is clear enough: Sentences have become easier to read. That trend is helpful to you as an effective writer. It means that in addition to being easier to read, short, readable sentences are increasingly familiar and culturally accepted.

One reason why short sentences are easier to read than longer ones may be that the longer sentences often incorporate more than one idea. Readers are taught to make sense of each sentence before moving on to the next. Eye-tracking studies can capture this process in action. Readers' eyes pause when they reach an end-of-sentence period, seemingly to process and integrate the sentence.[37] The period at the end of a sentence indicates that a certain unified concept is now complete. Readers then take a brief pause, process, and make sure they understand the completed sentence before moving on. Longer sentences require readers to hold more content in their minds before they process the full sentence—a more demanding cognitive task, especially if the sentence contains multiple independent ideas.

TWO US PRESIDENTIAL INAUGURAL ADDRESSES: OPENING FIVE SENTENCES[38]

	George Washington, 1789	Joseph Biden, 2021
1.	Among the vicissitudes incident to life, no event could have filled me with greater anxieties than that of which the notification was transmitted by your order, and received on the fourteenth day of the present month. (36 WORDS)	This is America's day. (4 WORDS)
2.	On the one hand, I was summoned by my Country, whose voice I can never hear but with veneration and love, from a retreat which I had chosen with the fondest predilection, and, in my flattering hopes, with an immutable decision, as the asylum of my declining years: a retreat which was rendered every day more necessary as well as more dear to me, by the addition of habit to inclination, and of frequent interruptions in my health to the gradual waste committed on it by time. (87 WORDS)	This is democracy's day. (4 WORDS)
3.	On the other hand, the magnitude and difficulty of the trust to which the voice of my Country called me, being sufficient to awaken in the wisest and most experienced of her citizens, a distrustful scrutiny into his qualifications, could not but overwhelm with despondence, one, who, inheriting inferior endowments from nature and unpractised in the duties of civil administration, ought to be peculiarly conscious of his own deficiencies. (69 WORDS)	A day of history and hope. (6 WORDS)
4.	In this conflict of emotions, all I dare aver, is, that it has been my faithful study to collect my duty from a just appreciation of every circumstance, by which it might be affected. (34 WORDS)	Of renewal and resolve. (4 WORDS)
5.	All I dare hope, is, that, if in executing this task, I have been too much swayed by a grateful remembrance of former instances, or by an affectionate sensibility to this transcendent proof, of the confidence of my fellow-citizens; and have thence too little consulted my incapacity as well as disinclination for the weighty and untried cares before me; my error will be palliated by the motives which misled me, and its consequences be judged by my Country, with some share of the partiality in which they originated. (89 WORDS)	Through a crucible for the ages America has been tested anew and America has risen to the challenge. (18 WORDS)

Consider what would have happened if we had combined the first two sentences of this section:

Separated: *We've already seen the benefits of using fewer words. But even if we hold the total number of words constant, writing shorter sentences usually makes a message easier to read.*

Combined: *We've already seen the benefits of using fewer words, but even if we hold the total number of words constant, writing shorter sentences usually makes a message easier to read.*

The *Separated* sentences contain thirty words, two sentences, and two ideas; each sentence has one main idea. Taken together, these sentences are written at an eighth-grade reading level. The *Combined* sentence uses the same thirty words, but they are combined into one long sentence. The text is still grammatically correct, but both ideas are now contained within a single sentence that the reader must process and keep track of while reading. Even though the *Combined* sentence uses the exact same words as the *Separated* sentences, its length makes it written at a college sophomore level.

THE RULES IN ACTION: WHAT READABLE WRITING LOOKS LIKE

Applying the rules of easy readability does not mean you are dumbing down your writing. Ernest Hemingway's *The Old Man and the Sea* is written at a fourth-grade reading level. In addition to being one of his most enduring works, it earned him a Nobel Prize in Literature—partly because his "simple" writing style contrasted with literary norms at the time.

Writing in a style that is easy to read is not necessarily easy to write. You might have to unlearn some of the overly formal and convoluted techniques that many of us were taught in high school and college. You might have to push back against colleagues, coauthors, or bosses who cling to the idea that complex writing automatically looks smarter or more professional. Using short and common words and writing with short and straightforward sentences requires extra time and attention. That investment is worth it, though, since none of our writing matters if people don't read it. And with practice, writing readably becomes easier.

Your training begins now, as we illustrate how revising for readability works. We will start with a complex sentence and apply each rule in turn. This example is taken from an article about the challenges posed by ballot initiatives, in which the public gets to vote directly on public policies.[39] (The article, ironically, was intended to call out the problem of obscure language!)

STARTING SENTENCE:
Often crafted from insidiously complicated language, designed to abstract contentious details, ballot measures are propagated as a tool of direct democracy in 24 states and Washington, D.C.

Apply rule 1: *Use short and common words.* We'll edit this sentence by replacing long and less common words with shorter and more common alternatives.

ILLUSTRATED:

*Often ~~crafted from insidiously complicated~~ **written with deceptively complex** language, designed to ~~abstract contentious~~ **hide controversial** details, ballot measures are ~~propagated~~ **used** as a tool of direct democracy in 24 states and Washington, D.C.*

EDITED:

Often written with deceptively complex language, designed to hide controversial details, ballot measures are used as a tool of direct democracy in 24 states and Washington, D.C.

Apply rule 2: *Write straightforward sentences.* We'll edit this sentence now by making it easy to understand in one pass, placing the important sentence elements next to each other.

ILLUSTRATED:

Often written with deceptively complex language, designed to hide controversial details, ballot measures are used as a tool of direct democracy in 24 states and Washington, D.C.

EDITED:

Ballot measures are used as a tool of direct democracy in 24 states and Washington, D.C., and are often written with deceptively complex language, designed to hide controversial details.

Finally, apply rule 3: *Write shorter sentences.* By separating the individual ideas, we make it easier for the reader to focus on the writer's central meaning.

ILLUSTRATED:

Ballot measures are used as a tool of direct democracy in 24 states and Washington, D.C.~~, and~~ ***They*** *are often written with deceptively complex language, designed to hide controversial details.*

EDITED:

Ballot measures are used as a tool of direct democracy in 24 states and Washington, D.C. They are often written with deceptively complex language, designed to hide controversial details.

Over the course of three steps we have gone from this:

Often crafted from insidiously complicated language, designed to abstract contentious details, ballot measures are propagated as a tool of direct democracy in 24 states and Washington, D.C.

To this:

Ballot measures are used as a tool of direct democracy in 24 states and Washington, D.C. They are often written with deceptively complex language, designed to hide controversial details.

Our original sentence was written at a level appropriate for someone with a graduate degree. The final sentence pair was written at a level appropriate for a tenth grader. It is more accessible to *all* readers, from those who struggle to read English to those who are simply too busy or distracted to recall instantly what "insidiously" means. In addition to being more likely to be understood, the final sentences also require less time and attention from the reader, which make them more likely to be read at all.

6

Third Principle: Design for Easy Navigation

One of the key aspects of writing for busy people is not strictly about writing at all. It is about *design*—specifically, designing the written content to be easy to navigate. When readers look at your message, they should immediately be able to grasp its purpose, main points, and structure. The way you place your words should help them quickly find the pieces they want to engage with, and the pieces they prefer to skip or skim.

To switch yourself into a navigation mindset, stop thinking of your message as a set of words and think of it instead as a type of map. Maps normally start from a zoomed-out perspective that allows you to orient yourself. When someone opens Google Maps, the default setting is a wide-scale, bird's-eye view of your current location. Printed paper maps similarly cover entire cities, states, or even countries. Think about a common map of the United States, either on paper or online. National borders, state lines, and labels clearly indicate which country you are looking at. Finer markings allow you to easily identify major lakes, cities, and other points of interest. Then you can zoom in for the details you want.

The way that readers approach writing has a lot in common with the way people use maps. They usually begin with a big-picture view, then decide to zoom in to parts that they think look most interesting or relevant. Think about your own reading process. Rather than reading the entire newspaper or scanning the entire homepage, you might skip directly to the local news or sports updates in the same way that you might zoom in to Utah and then in to Salt Lake City if you were planning a road trip there. Since busy readers don't typically read line by line, writing for easy, maplike navigation will help ensure that your readers notice and grasp the most important information before they move on.

Writers don't normally pay much attention to design, partly because of the way most of us were taught. Most likely, your English teacher talked a lot about grammar and transitions and supporting evidence in your writing, and very little about visual presentation. But letters, words, sentences, and paragraphs are intensely visual; they are literally *graphic elements* on the page or screen. It makes sense, then, that arranging those elements in a way that is pleasing and sensible to the eye will make the reading process easier.

Numerous studies demonstrate that refining the visual aspects of writing can make your messages significantly more effective. Sometimes we write better by focusing less on the words themselves, and more on how and where they appear.

THE RULES OF WELL-DESIGNED WRITING

Rule 1: Make Key Information Immediately Visible

The first question most of us ask when we see a map is, "What is this a map of?" Likewise, when we approach practical writing the first thing we ask is, "What is this about?" The easier writers make it for busy readers to orient themselves and answer that question, the more likely it is that those readers will engage and read the message.

The first step is making the key information instantly and explicitly clear. That might seem obvious, and yet writers fail to do it all the time. In the language of journalism, writing in a way that makes it hard to find the central point is called "burying the lede" (the word "lede" is a bit of newsroom jargon, with a deliberately odd spelling so it stands out). Sometimes writers bury the lede intentionally to spur curiosity and intrigue. *The New Yorker* is famous for stories that spend a lot of time establishing mood and setting before revealing the central idea or conflict. But practical communications aren't relaxed literary voyages, and they shouldn't be written like them.

Making the most important information immediately clear to the reader requires going back to basics and being equally clear about your own goals as a writer—this time with an added emphasis on visual presentation. Ask yourself again, "What do I want my readers to take away from this?" If your primary goal is for readers to attend a city council meeting, the meeting details and the request to attend should be the most obvious elements. But if you have multiple competing goals for a message, it can be challenging to figure out what the *key* information is that you want to highlight. In that case, you will have to figure out the hierarchy of your goals.

Imagine a CEO shares a memo with the board of directors to update them on the firm's progress on several critical items since the last corporate meeting. Within the update, the CEO also asks board members to recommend a consultant for an upcoming marketing project. The primary purpose of the memo is the update. The marketing consultant request is secondary. Somehow the presentation of the memo needs to convey that ranking of priorities.

There is no universal formula for *how* to make the most important information immediately clear. For communications that have titles and subject lines, these are good places to start. A subject line that reads "One action item after today's meeting" better conveys the email's key information than a subject line like "Today's meeting." But readable titles and subject lines are so short that they generally can only foreshadow key information rather than fully convey it.

A good rule of thumb, regardless of the specific type of communication, is to put the most important information in the places where busy readers most likely expect to find it. The US Army has codified this advice with a guideline that writers should place the *bottom line up front* (BLUF).[1] BLUF is an official army policy instructing writers to put the key information at the beginning of written communications. That way, readers in the army automatically know where to find the purpose of a communication.

Abstracts, executive summaries, and TL;DR headlines similarly function as "key information" locations for busy readers. At the same time, we should point out that the best way to apply this rule of thumb can vary widely across readers and cultures. We've heard anecdotally that the norm in some former Soviet republics is for the most important information to be in the final paragraph of official memos. Readers therefore often start skimming a memo from the bottom up. In contrast, the convention in many European Union countries is to place the most important information in the first paragraph (a European version of BLUF), so skimmers tend to work top-down.

There's an important insight here: Although the norms in two cultures may be different, readers in both contexts know where to look for the key information and writers know where to place it. These are culture-specific rules of thumb. Ultimately it is up to writers to structure their messages so that their particular readers can quickly orient and locate the key information. Part of doing so involves knowing where the readers expect that key information to be.

Not all contexts have clear norms, unfortunately. If a message is expected to be warm and friendly, the writing can come across as cold or aggressive if it begins immediately with the most important information. Consider the two examples on the next page. Readers of the *BLUF* version might be turned off by the directness of the message and view the writer as pushy or rude. On the other hand, if readers of the *Courteous Order* version quit before getting to the last line, they'll miss the key information. A middle-ground solution might include one sentence at the start to convey politeness, and then move into the ask: "I've thought more about our conversation. Can we set up a time to discuss you hiring my firm?"

Which approach works best? As with all the other principles we present, it depends both on your goals as a writer and on who your readers are.

COURTEOUS ORDER

Dear Potential Client:

I've thought more about our conversation. Your organization is not alone in facing the challenges we discussed. I think the services my firm offers could be of use to you.

Can we set up a time to discuss you hiring my firm?

Best,
Sales Associate

BOTTOM LINE UP FRONT (BLUF)

Dear Potential Client:

Can we set up a time to discuss you hiring my firm?

I've thought more about our conversation. Your organization is not alone in facing the challenges we discussed. I think the services my firm offers could be of use to you.

Best,
Sales Associate

Rule 2: Separate Distinct Ideas

Another way to help busy readers orient themselves quickly in the landscape of your writing is to separate distinct topics. Putting space between them makes it easier for the reader to skim and to scan for key information. A simple first step is to give each distinct topic its own paragraph, since a new paragraph visually signals a new set of ideas.

One of the most visually clear ways to signal to readers that ideas are distinct is to list each one with a bullet point. A study conducted in Denmark illustrates the benefits of using bullets or numbers to separate distinct topics.[2] A group of researchers recruited a representative sample of 888 adults to read a description of requirements for receiving unemployment benefits, using "bureaucratic language." Then the team tested whether changing how the information was presented—without adjusting the complexity of the language—affected a range of outcomes, including speed of reading and level of comprehension.

Around half of participants read a dense *Wall of Words* version, in which all the requirements were listed in a single continuous paragraph. The other half read the exact same content, but each distinct requirement was visually separated from the others using bullet points. These are the two versions:

WALL OF WORDS

Man kan søge om kontanthjælp, hvis man enten er over 30 år eller har en erhvervskompetencegivende uddannelse. Derudover gælder ifølge Lov om Aktiv Socialpolitik: Man skal jf. § 11 stk. 2 have været ude for en social begivenhed, fx sygdom, arbejdsløshed eller ophør af samliv. Ifølge § 11 stk. 2 skal den sociale begivenhed have medført, at man ikke kan skaffe det nødvendige til sig selv eller sin familie, og at man ikke kan forsørges af andre. Desuden skal behovet for forsørgelse skal ikke kunne dækkes af andre ydelser, fx dagpenge eller pension mv., jf. § 11 stk. 2. For at have ret til kontanthjælp skal man jf. § 11 stk. 3 lovligt have opholdt sig i riget i sammenlagt mindst 9 af de 10 seneste år, jf. dog stk. 4–10, og man skal ifølge § 11 stk. 8 have haft fuldtidsbeskæftigelse i riget i en periode svarende til 2 år og 6 måneder inden for de ti seneste år. Man skal være registreret som arbejdssøgende i jobcentret, jf. § 13b og hverken en selv eller ens eventuelle ægtefælle må have en formue, som kan dække deres økonomiske behov. Formue er fx penge og værdier, som let kan omsættes til penge. Kommunen ser dog bort fra beløb på op til 10.000 kr., for ægtefæller tilsammen op til 20.000 kr., jf. § 14 stk. 1, se dog undtagelser fra denne regel, jf. § 14 stk. 2–8 og stk. 15.

VISUALLY SEPARATED

Man kan søge om kontanthjælp, hvis man enten er over 30 år eller har en erhvervskompetencegivende uddannelse. Derudover gælder ifølge Lov om Aktiv Socialpolitik:

- Man skal jf. § 11 stk. 2 have været ude for en social begivenhed, fx sygdom, arbejdsløshed eller ophør af samliv.
- Ifølge § 11 stk. 2 skal den sociale begivenhed have medført, at man ikke kan skaffe det nødvendige til sig selv eller sin familie, og at man ikke kan forsørges af andre.
- Behovet for forsørgelse skal ikke kunne dækkes af andre ydelser, fx dagpenge eller pension mv., jf. § 11 stk. 2.
- Man skal jf. § 11 stk. 3 lovligt have opholdt sig i riget i sammenlagt mindst 9 af de 10 seneste år, jf. dog stk. 4–10.
- Ifølge § 11 stk. 8 skal man have haft fuldtidsbeskæftigelse i riget i en periode svarende til 2 år og 6 måneder inden for de ti seneste år.
- Man skal være registreret som arbejdssøgende i jobcentret, jf. § 13b.
- Hverken en selv eller ens eventuelle ægtefælle må have en formue, som kan dække deres økonomiske behov. Formue er fx penge og værdier, som let kan omsættes til penge. Kommunen ser dog bort fra beløb på op til 10.000 kr., for ægtefæller tilsammen op til 20.000 kr., jf. § 14 stk. 1, se dog undtagelser fra denne regel, jf. § 14 stk. 2–8 og stk. 15.

We cannot read Danish, which makes the difference between these two versions all the more stark. The *Wall of Words* version looks like it would be intimidating to read in any language. Both groups of participants understood the content similarly well, but those given the *Visually Separated* version read it ten seconds—or nearly 15%—faster than those given the *Wall of Words*.

Visually separating the topics made the writing easier to read, possibly because readers didn't have to spend time between sentences deciding whether they were related or distinct topics. Based on our experience, a numbered list or blank space or any other formatting technique to visually separate topics would have led to a comparable improvement.

Rule 3: Place Related Ideas Together

In addition to visually separating *distinct* ideas, placing *related* ideas next to each other (or as close as possible) can make it easier for readers to quickly grasp key information. The *Visually Separated* version of the Danish study described above follows this rule as well. Each distinct bullet point is related to one requirement for receiving unemployment benefits. Parsing them into separate bullets helps readers understand that they are individual requirements; keeping them next to each other helps readers understand that they are all related.

Imagine how much more confusing it would have been if the authors had inserted additional content unrelated to the unemployment benefits requirements between each of the bullets, such as information about how to apply for housing benefits. Readers focused on unemployment benefits would have had to search through all the bullet points to find the relevant ones. Busy readers would likely give up before finding the information they need.

Related ideas usually have related meanings, so placing them next to each other can make it possible to consolidate content and cut words. This "less is more" benefit can often be accomplished simply by reordering the text. Take the items listed below, about next steps for winning a proposal for a new contract:

- Jessie: Write client presentation slide deck based on past presentations
- Marion: Research competitors for this contract and any indication they are submitting proposals
- Jessie: Write proposed scope of work from codeveloped outline
- Marion: Research other public information about related products client has purchased in the past

Notice that Jessie has two items and Marion has two items. Placing Jessie's items next to each other and Marion's next to each other would help us more quickly find what we each need to do.

- Jessie: Write client presentation slide deck based on past presentations
- Jessie: Write proposed scope of work from codeveloped outline

- Marion: Research competitors for this contract and any indication they are submitting proposals
- Marion: Research other public information about related products client has purchased in the past

In this version, both of the tasks for Jessie involve writing, and both of the tasks for Marion involve research. The meaning of the tasks for Jessie and Marion can now be simplified and integrated. Doing this visually separates Jessie's to-do items from Marion's to-do items and cuts down on the total number of words from forty-six to thirty-nine, achieving several of this book's principles at once!

- @Jessie, write:
    - Client presentation slide deck based on past presentations
    - Proposed scope of work from codeveloped outline
- @Marion, research:
    - Competitors for this contract and any indication they are submitting proposals
    - Other public information about related products client has purchased in the past

Requests are a special type of information and require their own style of presentation. Often one message may contain multiple requests. Should the requests be grouped together or should they be separated and embedded throughout the message alongside related topics? The unsatisfactory answer is: It depends on the context. The guiding principle is that you want to make it as easy as possible for your readers to find and understand the requests. Doing so often entails combining many of the rules in this chapter.

If a message must contain multiple requests but they are all related to each other, it can be useful to group them next to each other (rule 3) and separate each individual request (rule 2). If the requests are all related to different topics that are covered in separate sections of the message, then it may make more sense to embed the requests with their relevant sections. In such cases, it can still be useful to foreshadow them as a group at the beginning of the message, like so: "Below I discuss my vacation preferences and ask for your opinion about: (1) Where should we go? (2) When should we go? (3) Who should we invite?" Presumably these three questions are also repeated in the related sections of the email. Redundancy is generally not ideal, but it can be an effective strategy to help busy readers understand multiple requests and to increase the likelihood that they will respond.

Formatting can also be a helpful tool for drawing attention to specific requests in a message, especially when they're scattered throughout. More on that a bit later.

Rule 4: Order Ideas by Priority

After deciding which ideas belong in your message, you have to choose the order in which you present them. Often there is underlying logic that dictates the order. Requests may make sense to order chronologically by when the action should be completed, or to order functionally based on how difficult they are to complete. If there is no clear logic to guide you, ordering decisions (as with everything else) should be informed by how readers read.

The first item in a list usually gets the most attention from the reader. One domain where this reading behavior has been studied is on election ballots, which commonly show long lists of candidates. An example of this research conducted on primary and runoff elections in Texas has shown that moving a candidate from last to first on a ballot can increase their share of the vote by nearly 10 percentage points in some races.[3] A likely explanation for this result is that voters begin reviewing candidates from the top of the ballot and work their way down from there. Once they find an acceptable candidate, they cast their vote and move on. Everyone is busy, even voters.

The multibillion-dollar internet-search advertising industry is built on a similar premise. The most valuable position in search results is at the top, because searchers tend to click on the first "good enough" option they see. Similarly, when Amazon wants to encourage sales of one item over another, it places that item before the others in your search results. Programmers at the company know that the first position is the one most likely to be seen, read, and acted on.

In certain contexts, the *last* position in an ordered list can also be influential—and not just in the regions of the former Soviet Union. Studies of jury trials have found that the final evidence presented to the jurors can be the most heavily weighted and remembered.[4] That said, jurors are ethically obliged to sit through an entire trial and hear all the evidence. When it comes to practical communications, busy readers are under no such obligation (no matter how compelling you might think your emails and memos are). That freedom to move on likely reduces how frequently they will encounter the last item in a list or extended message, and thus how influential that item is.

No single rule determines the best order for a message that contains multiple items or asks. When logic doesn't dictate the order, though, these behavioral patterns can help guide you. Whatever item is in the first position is likely to receive the most attention, and it's possible that the last spot is more likely to be read than the second-to-last spot. This is exactly what a group of business researchers found when they studied the effects of the order of links listed on a web page. They randomized the order of a half dozen links and found that the first position was clicked the most, with a steady decline in clicking with each position until the last position, where there was a small spike in clicking compared to the second-to-last position.[5]

Rule 5: Include Headings

You know exactly what we are about to discuss in this next section, right? It's hard to miss, since we just told you right above—in larger type, no less. Headings help busy readers scan a message and decide which parts they want to zoom in on, much the same way state names and boundaries do on a map of the US. Some common types of practical writing, such as text messages, don't have a place for headlines. But plenty of others do: emails, memos, sticky notes, to-do lists, and so on. Even tweets, Slack messages, and Facebook posts can begin with a few capitalized words that set up the idea to follow.

Headings are extremely useful in helping busy readers decide whether to move on or to pause, where to focus their attention, and how closely to read a certain section. Recall how people's eyes move as they search for relevant info, as shown in chapter 2:

☑ **Tip: The rubber impeller is located inside a stainless steel cup and uses the water for lubrication. If this water is not present, the friction of the rubber on stainless steel will very rapidly overheat and destroy the rubber impeller. This is why it's imperative NOT to operate, or even turn over, your outboard without there being a proper supply of water to the outboard beforehand.**

As a general rule, inspect the impeller and water pump assembly every year if operating in salt, brackish, or turbid water, and replace if necessary. The debris in these waters acts like sandpaper. If operating in freshwater that is clear and clean, this interval may likely stretch to two seasons, provided no dry operation has occurred. Be sure to check your particular owner's manual for your outboard's specific service interval.

☑ **Tip: If you're at all uneasy about performing impeller/water pump inspection and replacement procedures, have your local Yamaha Marine dealer do the work. They have the tools, materials, and training to do it right, for your peace of mind.**

Belts and Hoses

Any belts and hoses your outboard has have to operate in the brutally harsh marine environment. Give them a glance once in a while and heed the manufacturer's schedule for their replacement. If you find cracking or fraying, be safe and replace. Do not attempt to "flip" a belt in order to extend its life, nor should you handle the belt with lubricant of any kind on your fingers. Keep these safe from spray-on lubricants, too.

☑ **Tip: Yamaha four-stroke outboard timing belts and HDPI® two-stroke outboard high-pressure fuel pump belts are cogged and Kevlar®-impregnated, making them super-tough and non-stretchable. Still, Yamaha recommends they be changed every five years or every 1,000 hours.**

Spark Plugs

As a general rule, pull four-stroke outboard spark plugs every 200 hours or every other season and check for proper color and wear. They should be a light brownish color and have relatively sharp edges. When necessary, replace with the exact manufacturer and part number that your outboard's manufacturer stipulates. The brand type and style of spark plugs used in your outboard are by design. They contain specific performance attributes that are engineered into your outboard. Those little markings and numbers on your spark plugs contain a wealth of information about heat range, thread depth, etc.—so don't second-guess or try to cross-reference here. Your outboard's performance depends on it.

Air Intake Passages

Be sure to check the air intake passages for any obstructions such as bird nests and other debris brought in by various critters. Look under your cowling, too. It doesn't take long for your outboard or boat to become home to local birds and bugs, and it can be a real headscratcher when it comes to performance-loss diagnosis.

Thermostats and Pop-Off Valves

These are responsible for regulating the operating temperature of your outboard. Simple and effective, they're best observed through any signs of change in the engine's operating temperature. Operating in saltwater can cause deposits to build up, causing the valves to stick open, which can over-cool the outboard and prevent it from reaching proper operating temperature. Small bits of debris in the cooling water can get lodged between mating surfaces and cause the same condition. If this happens, removal and cleaning is most often the [illegible]. Check your owner's manual for specific replacement recommendations.

Notice how people's eyes skip to each heading?

In a study we conducted with the Journalist's Resource (separate from the one we mentioned in chapter 4), its writers put together a nine-paragraph email newsletter covering three topics: research on climate change and health, research on gun violence, and details about how to apply for a journalism award. For each topic, there were also links to additional content. Half of the newsletter's 46,648 subscribers received the nine-paragraph email with no headings. The other half received the same content, but with descriptive headings placed above the second topic (gun violence) and third topic (journalism award).[6]

Subscribers who received the email with the headings were more than twice as likely to click on links related to the second and third topics as were those who received the no-headings version. One might worry that the headings merely diverted readers away from the first topic toward the second and third, but that wasn't the case: There was no difference in reader engagement with the links in the first section (on climate change and health) between those who received the email with headings and those who received the one without. It seems that the headings helped busy readers quickly find more interesting topics that they otherwise would have skipped over.

For more evidence of how useful headings can be, consider a letter we helped a school district redesign during the Covid pandemic. Its aim was to alert parents that someone at their child's school had contracted Covid and that a range of protocols had been set in motion. One of these protocols was that the school would be closed for at least the next forty-eight hours, effective as soon as the letter was sent.

The school district's leader asked us to review their letter and make suggestions for improvement. Since we had little context, we didn't edit any of the words. We focused solely on designing the letter for navigability.

ORIGINAL

Dear [SCHOOL DISTRICT NAME] Families and Staff,

Today the district was informed that an individual with COVID-19 was at [SCHOOL NAME] while potentially infectious. By law, we must maintain this person's confidentiality, which prevents us from further identifying the individual and his/her reason for being in the school. We are working collaboratively with the [COUNTY NAME] Department of Health to identify any students and staff who may have been in contact with this person.

We will take the following actions:

- [SCHOOL NAME] will initially remain closed for 48 hours.
- [SCHOOL NAME] is the only building closing on [DATE] and [DATE].
- [SCHOOL NAME] will deliver instruction virtually this week on [DATE] and [DATE].
- The school building will be disinfected following DOH and CDC guidelines.
- The school will begin contact tracing that will be communicated to the department of health.

The [COUNTY NAME] Department of Health has a contact-tracing system in place for [COUNTY NAME] when there is a confirmed case of COVID-19. The intent is to identify those who have been in close contact with a positive person. Close contact means being within six feet of a person with COVID-19 for more than 10 minutes.

If your child is identified as a close contact of the person who tested positive, you will receive a call from a contact tracer. For such calls, your caller ID may read [STATE NAME] Contact Tracing or display a phone number with a [###] area code. Please answer these calls promptly and provide the Contact Tracers with the information they need to protect us all. Individuals who were in close contact must be quarantined for 14 days from the last exposure date and should monitor for symptoms.

Furthermore, the district will also send emails to families notifying them if their children have been identified as having contact with an individual that is positive. If you do not receive an email in the next 48 hours, your child is NOT believed to have any risk of exposure.

As a reminder, if you believe at any point you and/or your child may have been in close contact with someone who has COVID-19, you and/or your child should self-quarantine and be tested.

If you suspect your child is becoming ill, your child should stay home. Symptoms of COVID-19 are listed on the CDC website: https://www.cdc.gov/coronavirus/2019-ncov/symptoms-testing/symptoms.html. You should consult with your physician for medical advice.

Visit the [STATE NAME] Find a Test Site Near You page at [LINK] to find a list of testing sites. If you go to a testing site run by [STATE NAME], the test is free. For more information on COVID-19, please call (888) 123-4567 or visit the [STATE NAME] Department of Health homepage.

Please know that we will be transparent about any COVID-19 cases in our district, and we will keep you informed. Please contact your child's school administrators or 555-555-5555 ext. 1234 if you have any additional questions or concerns.

Sincerely, [SUPERINTENDENT NAME]

WITH HEADINGS

Dear [SCHOOL DISTRICT NAME] Families and Staff,

[SCHOOL NAME] will be closed for at least the next 48 hours.

Today the district was informed that an individual with COVID-19 was at [SCHOOL NAME] while potentially infectious. By law, we must maintain this person's confidentiality, which prevents us from further identifying the individual and his/her reason for being in the school. We are working collaboratively with the [COUNTY NAME] Department of Health to identify any students and staff who may have been in contact with this person.

What is [SCHOOL NAME] doing?

We will take the following actions:

- [SCHOOL NAME] will initially remain closed for 48 hours.
- [SCHOOL NAME] is the only building closing on [DATE] and [DATE].
- [SCHOOL NAME] will deliver instruction virtually this week on [DATE] and [DATE].
- The school building will be disinfected following DOH and CDC guidelines.
- The school will begin contact tracing that will be communicated to the department of health.

How will you know if your child is a close contact?

The [COUNTY NAME] Department of Health has a contact tracing system in place for [COUNTY NAME] when there is a confirmed case of COVID-19. The intent is to identify those who have been in close contact with a positive person. Close contact means being within six feet of a person with COVID-19 for more than 10 minutes.

If your child is identified as a close contact of the person who tested positive, you will receive a call from a contact tracer. For such calls, your caller ID may read [STATE NAME] Contact

Tracing or display a phone number with a [###] area code. Please answer these calls promptly and provide the Contact Tracers with the information they need to protect us all. Individuals who were in close contact must be quarantined for 14 days from the last exposure date and should monitor for symptoms.

Furthermore, the district will also send emails to families notifying them if their children have been identified as having contact with an individual that is positive. If you do not receive an email in the next 48 hours, your child is NOT believed to have any risk of exposure.

As a reminder, if you believe at any point you and/or your child may have been in close contact with someone who has COVID-19, you and/or your child should self-quarantine and be tested.

What to do if you or your child is sick?

If you suspect your child is becoming ill, your child should stay home. Symptoms of COVID-19 are listed on the CDC website: https://www.cdc.gov/coronavirus/2019-ncov/symptoms-testing/symptoms.html. You should consult with your physician for medical advice.

Visit the [STATE NAME] Find a Test Site Near You page at [LINK] to find a list of testing sites. If you go to a testing site run by [STATE NAME], the test is free. For more information on COVID-19, please call (888) 123-4567 or visit the [STATE NAME] Department of Health homepage.

Please know that we will be transparent about any COVID-19 cases in our district, and we will keep you informed. Please contact your child's school administrators or 555-555-5555 ext. 1234 if you have any additional questions or concerns.

Sincerely, [SUPERINTENDENT NAME]

We put ourselves in the mindset of the intended reader. Imagine being a busy parent with school-aged children at home asking for help with their homework and wanting to know when dinner will be ready. You receive the *Original* version of the email in your inbox and hastily look it over between putting chicken tenders in the oven and stirring the pasta. Would you read closely enough to realize school is closed for the next two days? Probably not. You would probably be even less likely to grasp many of the specific details about quarantine protocols. The *Original* letter looks so impenetrable that you might just postpone reading it at all.

Now consider the redesigned *With Headings* version of the school email. To improve ease of navigation, we applied our own rules. We made the key information immediately clear (rule 1) by declaring at the top that "[SCHOOL NAME] will be closed for at least the next 48 hours." We then added headings for each distinct topic and section, allowing parents to navigate to whichever topics they were most interested in and had time for. Although we were not able to test the impact of this version, we are confident that the revised layout was more effective because it was easier to navigate.

Headings can be useful even for prefacing lists. As we've discussed, bullet points can help with organizing content and improving navigability. But just because an idea is tied to a bullet point doesn't automatically make it clear and easy to understand. We've all seen messages that have full paragraphs attached to each bullet point or that contain so many bulleted items that it's hard to tell what they all have in common. In such cases, including a short heading at the beginning of each bulleted idea can offer a helpful guide for readers, especially if each bullet point is unrelated to the others. For instance, imagine an email to a colleague about two distinct items:

- <u>Revised contract</u>: The firm's lawyers have agreed to all of our proposed edits to the contract but have requested the addition of two final clauses. Can you please review these additions to see if they're acceptable?
- <u>Conference planning</u>: We're just about three months away from the conference date, so we should start finalizing the list of invited participants and the program of events. Could we set up a call to discuss next steps?

The short headings attached to each bullet help readers quickly understand what items are included in the list.

In general, headings should be just long and detailed enough to clearly describe what the subsequent content is about, but not so long as to impose an additional reading burden. If a reader can understand an entire section based just on the heading, the heading is probably too long. In the school letter mentioned earlier, "What is [SCHOOL NAME] doing?" is more helpful and descriptive than "Next steps." But a heading of "[SCHOOL NAME] is monitoring all close contacts, and closing and disinfecting the building" would be unnecessarily long and detailed. Many busy readers might not ever register the full meaning of that message if it were crammed into the subject line of an email.

Rule 6: Consider Using Visuals

Effective writing, by definition, relies on words, sentences, and paragraphs to convey ideas. But effective *communication* doesn't have to abide by that constraint. As editor in chief of *Time* magazine, Nancy Gibbs would often write a note to her staff in the margins of articles she was editing: "Is this best conveyed with words?" Despite being a masterful writer, she knew that words aren't always best for quickly and efficiently delivering information to busy readers.

Remember the catchy street sign that our student proposed?

Much as we liked the way our student improved on the wordiness of the original sign, we realized that an image could convey the exact same message more quickly and more universally without using any words at all:

Conveying critical information visually is also beneficial when there are language barriers. Someone who doesn't speak French would still immediately understand this sign:

It's not often that we can or should transform a practical message into a completely wordless graphic. But there are many less extreme ways that pictures and images can be useful to the reader. Many communications can be made more effective by converting some sentences into tables or graphics.

Line graphs and bar graphs are simple, effective tools for conveying quantitative information, such as measurement or performance trends. Infographics can help convey nonquantitative information, such as the steps required to assemble a piece of furniture. Effective graphics don't have to consolidate all relevant information into a single graph or image. Rather, they can serve to simplify communication. For a deep and inspiring discussion of ways to share ideas graphically, we recommend starting with Edward Tufte's classic book *The Visual Display of Quantitative Information*.

Even simple tables that arrange words and numbers within a framework can convey complex ideas much more clearly than can words alone. The advice to use these types of visuals when possible is part of the Federal Plain Language Guidelines, the set of rules designed to make sure that US government documents are comprehensible to the general public. The following example is taken directly from those guidelines:[7]

ORIGINAL:

We must receive your completed application form on or before the 15th day of the second month following the month you are reporting if you do not submit your application electronically or the 25th day of the second month following the month you are reporting if you submit your application electronically.

VISUALLY DISPLAYED:

If you submit your form . . .	**We must receive it by . . .**
Electronically	the 25th of the second month following the month you are reporting
Other than electronically	the 15th of the second month following the month you are reporting

Notice how the *Visually Displayed* version is easy to skim, whereas following the first requires reading it more closely. With the *Visually Displayed* version, if you want to submit an application electronically, you don't need to read the last row of the table at all; you can just navigate immediately to the first row ("Electronically"). And vice versa if you do not submit electronically. The *Original* and *Visually Displayed* versions both include the same content, but the latter leverages the logic of tables to reduce the effort required to understand the information.

THE RULES IN ACTION: WHAT GOOD NAVIGATION LOOKS LIKE

To see how these rules can be applied to real communication with meaningful consequences, we turn to a study conducted by a research team that worked with the New York Police Department to redesign the city's court summons notifications.[8] In New York City, people who commit low-level offenses are issued a paper summons to appear in court at a specified date and time. If they miss their court date, a warrant can be issued for their arrest. Despite the threat, many recipients fail to appear at their scheduled court hearing.

Failure to appear in court tends to be interpreted by law enforcement and lawyers as an active decision—that is, that the recipients intentionally *decided* to not appear for court. In a 2020 study, a team of researchers questioned that assumption. They investigated whether many people fail to appear simply because the written summons is difficult to understand.

The standard court summons used by the NYPD at the time of the study is shown on the next page. It was titled "Complaint/ Information." The first two-thirds of the notification listed details about the arrested person and about the charges levied against them. The recipient had to get to the bottom of the form to find

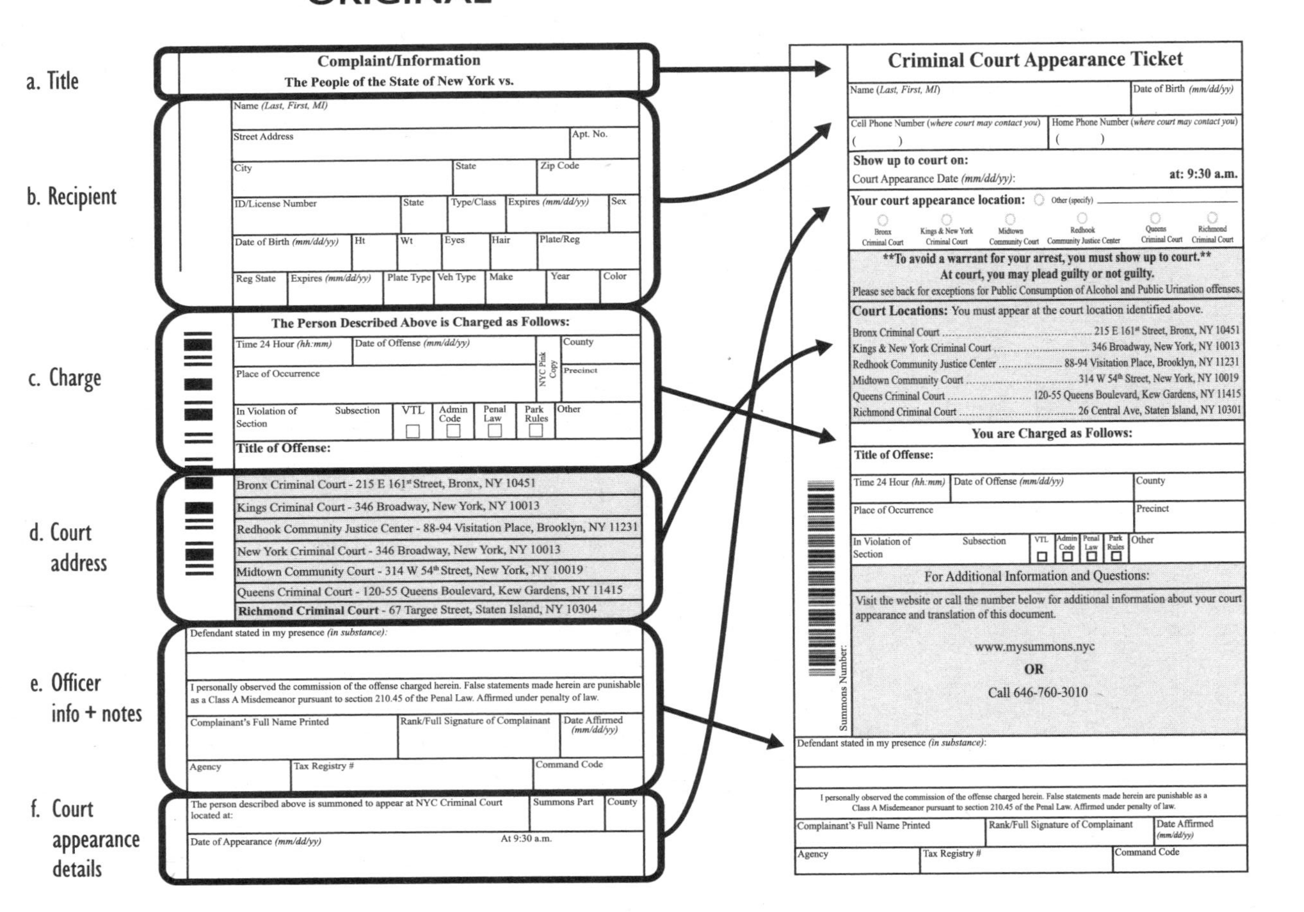
ORIGINAL
DESIGNED FOR NAVIGABILITY
a. Title
b. Recipient
c. Charge
d. Court address
e. Officer info + notes
f. Court appearance details
Complaint/Information
The People of the State of New York vs.
Name (Last, First, MI)
Street Address
Apt. No.
City
State
Zip Code
ID/License Number
State
Type/Class
Expires (mm/dd/yy)
Sex
Date of Birth (mm/dd/yy)
Ht
Wt
Eyes
Hair
Plate/Reg
Reg State
Expires (mm/dd/yy)
Plate Type
Veh Type
Make
Year
Color
The Person Described Above is Charged as Follows:
Time 24 Hour (hh:mm)
Date of Offense (mm/dd/yy)
NYC Pink Copy
County
Place of Occurrence
Precinct
In Violation of Section
Subsection
VTL
Admin Code
Penal Law
Park Rules
Other
Title of Offense:
Bronx Criminal Court - 215 E 161st Street, Bronx, NY 10451
Kings Criminal Court - 346 Broadway, New York, NY 10013
Redhook Community Justice Center - 88-94 Visitation Place, Brooklyn, NY 11231
New York Criminal Court - 346 Broadway, New York, NY 10013
Midtown Community Court - 314 W 54th Street, New York, NY 10019
Queens Criminal Court - 120-55 Queens Boulevard, Kew Gardens, NY 11415
Richmond Criminal Court - 67 Targee Street, Staten Island, NY 10304
Defendant stated in my presence (in substance):
I personally observed the commission of the offense charged herein. False statements made herein are punishable as a Class A Misdemeanor pursuant to section 210.45 of the Penal Law. Affirmed under penalty of law.
Complainant's Full Name Printed
Rank/Full Signature of Complainant
Date Affirmed (mm/dd/yy)
Agency
Tax Registry #
Command Code
The person described above is summoned to appear at NYC Criminal Court located at:
Summons Part
County
Date of Appearance (mm/dd/yy)
At 9:30 a.m.
Criminal Court Appearance Ticket
Name (Last, First, MI)
Date of Birth (mm/dd/yy)
Cell Phone Number (where court may contact you)
Home Phone Number (where court may contact you)
Show up to court on:
Court Appearance Date (mm/dd/yy):
at: 9:30 a.m.
Your court appearance location:
Other (specify)
Bronx Criminal Court
Kings & New York Criminal Court
Midtown Community Court
Redhook Community Justice Center
Queens Criminal Court
Richmond Criminal Court
To avoid a warrant for your arrest, you must show up to court.
At court, you may plead guilty or not guilty.
Please see back for exceptions for Public Consumption of Alcohol and Public Urination offenses.
Court Locations: You must appear at the court location identified above.
Bronx Criminal Court .... 215 E 161st Street, Bronx, NY 10451
Kings & New York Criminal Court .... 346 Broadway, New York, NY 10013
Redhook Community Justice Center .... 88-94 Visitation Place, Brooklyn, NY 11231
Midtown Community Court .... 314 W 54th Street, New York, NY 10019
Queens Criminal Court .... 120-55 Queens Boulevard, Kew Gardens, NY 11415
Richmond Criminal Court .... 26 Central Ave, Staten Island, NY 10301
You are Charged as Follows:
Title of Offense:
Time 24 Hour (hh:mm)
Date of Offense (mm/dd/yy)
County
Place of Occurrence
Precinct
In Violation of Section
Subsection
VTL
Admin Code
Penal Law
Park Rules
Other
For Additional Information and Questions:
Visit the website or call the number below for additional information about your court appearance and translation of this document.
www.mysummons.nyc
OR
Call 646-760-3010
Summons Number:
Defendant stated in my presence (in substance):
I personally observed the commission of the offense charged herein. False statements made herein are punishable as a Class A Misdemeanor pursuant to section 210.45 of the Penal Law. Affirmed under penalty of law.
Complainant's Full Name Printed
Rank/Full Signature of Complainant
Date Affirmed (mm/dd/yy)
Agency
Tax Registry #
Command Code

the most critical information: the fact that they were expected to show up to a specific court on a specific date at a specific time.

For their study, the researchers redesigned the form to make it more visually accessible. Their new version employed all the rules of navigability that we have laid out in this chapter.

First, they made the purpose of the form immediately clear (rule 1) and placed that information up top (rule 4). They changed the title from "Complaint/Information," which gives no indication of what the communication is, to the unambiguous "Criminal Court Appearance Ticket." At the top of the notice, they also added the relevant details regarding where and when the recipient was required to appear. Any reader who starts at the top of the redesigned notice is likely to immediately understand that they are being asked to appear at a particular court on a particular date. Even if they then stop reading, they will have grasped this key information.

Second, the researchers visually separated distinct topics (rule 2). In the *Original* version, the officer information (e) and the details about showing up to court (f) are next to each other and formatted similarly. A busy reader might think they are related, but in reality they are completely different topics. The *Designed for Navigability* version separates these items, moving the court appearance details (f) to the top of the form.

Third, the modified version puts related topics next to each other (rule 3) by placing in one location all the information needed to appear in court: the court address (d), along with the date and time (f).

Fourth, the researchers added headings (rule 5). Most notably, they added clear headings to highlight the court appearance details (f), flagging them with the words "Show up to court on" and "Your court appearance location."

Fifth, the courthouse details (f) in the *Original* version require the officer to hand-write the name of the specific courthouse at which the citizen is to appear. This could lead to misunderstanding and failure to appear in court if the officer's handwriting is illegible. The *Designed for Navigability* version visually displays this element (rule 6) with the courthouses listed horizontally. All the officer has to do is fill in the appropriate bubble.

The researchers then tested the impact of the redesigned form over a seventeen-month period in which nearly 324,000 residents received one of the two summonses. Failure-to-appear rates were 13% lower among residents who received the redesigned form compared to residents who received the older form. Based on that rate, the researchers estimate that the *Designed for Navigability* version resulted in some twenty-three thousand fewer arrest warrants being issued. The better-designed form spared those defendants the escalating consequences of failing to appear in court, and avoided further involving an already overextended justice system. It is now the standard summons citywide.

While not many of us regularly write (or read) court summonses, everyone can benefit from these same principles of designing for easy navigation. Getting in touch with your inner mapmaker can help you become much more effective at connecting with busy readers.

7

Fourth Principle: Use Enough Formatting but No More

Formatting is a bit like spices when cooking: You want to include them thoughtfully, and you don't want to use too much. In that spirit, try to think of underlining, bolding, italics, all caps ("all capitals"), bullets, and other text manipulations not just as tools but as functional ingredients you can add to your writing.

The standard formatting tools that we use today are the result of millennia of experimentation and innovation. In the early days of Roman-Saxon writing, writers did not use punctuation or even spaces between words. Then a set of enterprising Irish scribes in the seventh century CE began "aerating" text with spaces to make reading easier.[1] You can see what a breakthrough that was:

Nonaerated: *Centurieslaterspacesbetweenwordsbecamecanonical.*
Aerated: *Centuries later spaces between words became canonical.*

Apparently writers were worried about getting through to busy readers back then, too. Spaces make reading *a lot* easier and faster. (We salute you, Irish scribes.) Eventually line breaks—what we now recognize as paragraphs—were consistently used to mark the ends and beginnings of ideas. Then came italics, highlighting, bolding, and so on. Today, we're accustomed to seeing writing that uses a range of formatting to help readers understand and navigate texts.

Formatting serves two main purposes. First, it conveys meaning over and above the meaning of the words themselves. Second, formatting helps capture readers' attention by making certain words stand out against the others.

Remember how visual contrast automatically draws the viewer's attention? Let's revisit our park scene:

In the same way the person walking the dog contrasts with their surroundings in this image, formatted words contrast with nearby nonformatted words, and so they are often noticed first. This highly noticeable contrast makes formatting a potent tool for writers who want to draw readers' attention to specific information or ideas.

Once readers have noticed the formatted words, they apply their own rules of thumb to make sense of the formatting. For instance, ALL CAPS are commonly interpreted as shouting, and *italics* sometimes come across as ironic or snarky, and other times as simply emphasized. A notable challenge here is that the rules readers use don't always align with writers' intended meaning. As a result, understanding readers' rules is critical for writers who want to use formatting effectively.

THE RULES OF EFFECTIVE FORMATTING

Rule 1: Match Formatting to Readers' Expectations

To uncover the typical ways that readers interpret different types of formatting, we conducted an online survey. We asked 797 people what they think writers mean when they use various common styles of formatting. To keep the question neutral, we provided no guidance or preselected response options. We simply asked respondents to share their interpretations.[2]

Highlighting, <u>underlining</u>, **bolding**

The vast majority of people who responded to our survey reported that they interpret **bolded**, <u>underlined</u>, and highlighted text as indicating the things that the writer believes are most important. Note that text messages and social media posts generally do not support these types of formatting. Writers who are communicating through those channels have more limited options, putting more emphasis strictly on the words themselves.

ITALICS AND FONT COLOR

When it comes to *italics* and changes in **font color**, readers have divergent interpretations. Some interpret both italics and font colors as tools for directing attention to the most important information, but others interpret them as conveying a more narrow emphasis within a sentence. This is a subtle but important distinction. Sometimes writers want to make a word or phrase stand out from the surrounding text in order to deepen the meaning of that text; that is *emphasis*. (See what we just did?) Think about the sentence "I am very excited for our upcoming convening" versus "I am *very* excited for our upcoming convening." In the latter sentence, "very" is not the most important word, but it *is* emphasized to underscore the extent of the writer's excitement.

Because importance and emphasis are not the same, and because readers may interpret italics and font colors as conveying either of those meanings, writers who want to use these tools need to be careful to manage their ambiguity. Some professions and professional organizations have established norms for the use of different types of formatting, which reduces the potential for confusion. In legal writing, for instance, italics are typically used when referring to previous cases being cited. But in settings where such norms don't already exist, writers may want to provide context that helps readers interpret their formatting choices.

Writers can announce their style up front—for instance, "The most important points are in blue" or "I've italicized the most important points." Such explicit statements create norms for readers, similar to the way textbooks frequently display key concepts in a different font color and define the significance of the color at the beginning or end of each chapter. Writers can also add headers (such as "Most important:") before bolded or italicized sentences to remove any uncertainty. But, as noted earlier, writers who communicate through text messages or social media generally don't have the option of italics and font color, either. They are therefore more likely to use all caps or the quintessential modern formatting embellishment, the emoji.

ALL CAPITAL LETTERS (ALL CAPS)

A majority of survey respondents also interpreted all caps as signaling importance, but a sizable fraction (25%) volunteered that they regarded all caps as conveying anger instead. The latter interpretation probably reflects the rise of social media, where capitalized comments are often considered aggressive or even hostile. If a formatting type has more than one common interpretation, it can cause confusion. When a reader sees a sentence in all caps, they may pause to wonder: Is the writer angry, or is the writer underscoring that these words are important? Or both? Careful reading of the surrounding content may help readers sort out the writer's true intention, but many busy readers will have already quit by then.

Perhaps because of these ambiguities, all-caps use has been a subject of legal deliberation. The US Federal Trade Commission requires that consumer disclosures (such as legal terms and conditions) be "clear and conspicuous."[3] To satisfy the requirement, many organizations use all caps in critical sections of contracts; for instance, more than three-quarters of the terms-and-conditions contracts for Amazon, Uber, and Facebook contain at least one all-caps paragraph.[4] Some state laws explicitly mandate that all caps must be used to highlight key sections in specific types of agreements, ranging from child-support orders to explanations of eviction rights.[5] But given the varied ways that readers interpret formatting, rather than ensuring specific words are read, using all caps might effectively hide them in plain sight.

Recognizing this possibility, some courts have recently determined that all-caps text is not sufficient for informing consumers about critical content in disclosures and legal statements.[6] Research has backed up the courts' opinion. Studies show that all-caps text does not enhance readers' understanding. Capitalized passages take significantly longer to read than normal text, especially for older adults, and it can actually decrease comprehension.[7]

One broad upside of the all-caps option is that it is available to writers in any medium, from paper to email to web forms to office chats. Unlike most other formatting types, capitalization is also feasible in text messages and social media posts. Just keep in mind that all caps can be used to indicate emphasis, but they can even more readily be taken as impolite or childish shouting. Be careful to make sure your audience thinks you mean what *you* think you mean.

BULLETS

Bullets are extremely useful formatting tools, though they, too, suffer from mixed interpretations. They also typically do not translate well to social media or text messaging. Most of the respondents to our survey indicated that bulleted items broadly signify important content, but a substantial proportion specifically interpreted bulleted items as signaling lists that follow a hierarchy and logic. In the latter view, the words conveyed with bullets are logically connected to each other and to the phrase that preceded the bullets.

In general, readers look to the sentence preceding a bulleted list to determine whether the list itself is worth reading. If you intend the list to follow a hierarchy, that would be the logical place to tell the reader. Readers also widely recognize that subbullets—bullets that are indented and nested under higher-level bullets—are related to the higher-level bullet immediately above them. Consequently, readers may skip over the subbullets if the higher-level bullet point is not relevant to them.

The US government's Federal Plain Language Guidelines illustrates how useful bullets can be for organizing and simplifying information, helping readers to more quickly understand key points. The guidelines show two versions of a description of Medicaid eligibility criteria as an example.[8]

STANDARD:

Medicaid: Apply if you are aged (65 years old or older), blind, or disabled and have low income and few resources. Apply if you are terminally ill and want to receive hospice services. Apply if you are aged, blind, or disabled; live in a nursing home; and have low income and limited resources. Apply if you are aged, blind, or disabled and need nursing home care, but can stay at home with special community care services. Apply if you are eligible for Medicare and have low income and limited resources.

BULLETED:

You may apply for Medicaid if you are:

- *Terminally ill and want hospice services*
- *Eligible for Medicare and have low income and limited resources*
- *65 years old or older, blind, or disabled and have low income and few resources and:*
    - *Live in a nursing home*
    - *Need nursing home care but can stay at home with special community care services*

The *Standard* and *Bulleted* versions convey the exact same content, but the latter is much easier and quicker to read exactly because it organizes the information in a way that readers expect and understand. Each bullet connects to the sentence that precedes the bulleted list, and each subbullet relates to the higher-level bullet above it.

The varied ways that readers interpret bullets mean that they need to be used carefully. Writers often use bulleted lists to organize content but without intending to imply that the bulleted items are more important than surrounding ideas that are not bulleted. For instance, an organization we work with shared an email written by its chairperson to other board members. One of the primary goals of the message was to find a time to schedule the next board meeting; this key question was embedded in a paragraph at the end of the message. But the message also included six paragraphs of other information, including a bulleted list of thirteen items that new clients received from the organization, such as chocolate, caramels, and a plant. We didn't write the message, but it seems safe to assume that the bulleted list of gifts for new clients was less important than the question on scheduling the next meeting.

In such cases, bullets can create a clash between the reader's goals and the writer's. If readers infer that a bulleted list is also the most important part of your message, they may feel entitled to bypass the rest of the message after reading the bulleted items, thereby missing whatever information you actually wanted to convey as most important. Sure enough, after the chairperson sent the message described above, they had trouble scheduling the next meeting.

Using bullet points to list low-priority items risks misdirecting the reader away from what truly matters. Listing the items in a single sentence, separated by semicolons, might have prevented busy board members from missing the more important information elsewhere in the document.

Busy readers should never need to stop and question what you mean by the bolded (or italicized, highlighted, underlined, etc.) text. You can head off that confusion by understanding your readers' interpretations or by being explicit about your own. Once the writer and readers agree on the meanings, formatting can be highly effective for making messages easy to read, understand, and engage with.

Rule 2: Highlight, **Bold**, or Underline the Most Important Ideas

Since the vast majority of people interpret highlighted, bolded, and underlined text as identifying what the writer thinks is most important, these tools are useful for drawing readers' attention to critical portions of the text.

In another of our online studies, we paid a group of more than 1,600 participants to read a five-paragraph passage. Right in the middle of the fourth paragraph, we embedded a sentence that instructed readers to select "Busy readers" as an answer to a later survey question. Some participants were shown a version of the passage that had no formatting. Among that first group, 65% followed the instructions; they spent an average of almost two minutes reading the passage. The rest of the participants saw the same passage, but with the instructional sentence either highlighted in yellow, underlined, or bolded. In the second group, 89% followed the instructions—and they spent almost twenty fewer seconds reading, on average.[9] Formatting the key words captured the readers' attention, communicated the desired message, and reduced the amount of time readers spent on the rest of the passage.

Because these formatting types are so effective, they can have an important unintended consequence: They will easily draw readers' attention away from everything else. In an earlier, 2021 study, we asked nearly one thousand people to read the same five-paragraph passage.[10] In the middle of the fourth paragraph, we instructed them to select a specific response option to a later survey question to earn a bonus equal to half of their compensation for participating in the study.

Among those assigned to read the passage with no formatting, 48% followed the instructions and earned the bonus. Another group was presented with an irrelevant sentence highlighted. In this case, only 39% read the (unhighlighted) instructional sentence and selected the correct response option to receive their extra compensation. Perhaps because participants believed the writer had intentionally formatted the most important information, they read the rest of the text less closely than they would have if none of the text had been formatted at all.[11]

The key message here is that highlighting, bolding, and underlining involve trade-offs: They increase the likelihood that readers read the formatted words, but they can decrease the reading of everything else. Used well, these tools can help readers locate and understand the most important information. But used ineffectively, they can undermine writers' goals. As with all aspects of effective writing, you need to know your reader and you need to know your goals.

Rule 3: Limit Your Formatting

As with words, ideas, and requests, less is more when it comes to formatting, too. In another version of the nearly one-thousand-person study we just described, we again showed our online survey participants a five-paragraph passage with the embedded instructional sentence in the fourth paragraph.[12] As before, participants who were assigned to read the passage with the embedded instructions highlighted were more likely to follow through and earn a bonus than participants who saw the same passage with no formatting. No surprise, right? Highlighted writing is more likely to be read.

But this time, we added a new condition in which participants saw the same passage with *five* highlighted sentences, including the embedded instructional sentence. Participants in this group, who saw four sentences highlighted in addition to the instructional sentence, were less likely to earn the bonus than participants who saw only the instructional sentence highlighted. Overall, 84% of participants in the group that saw a single highlighted sentence earned the bonus, compared to just 65% of participants who saw five highlighted sentences. Highlighting five sentences still yielded a better response than highlighting none (55% success rate), but formatting multiple items in the same passage evidently diluted the benefit by spreading busy readers' attention across all the formatted items.

The broad takeaway is to avoid formatting multiple items when you particularly want your reader to focus on just one. Sometimes you really do want the reader to focus on more than one place, however. We are often asked, "What should I do if I have three (or more) important items that all need to be addressed in the same message?" Our first response tends to be asking whether all the information genuinely is important. If the answer is yes, we then ask whether all the information needs to be included in a single message. If the answer is yes again, the writer now has to be extremely judicious in applying formatting. (We discuss this issue in greater detail in chapter 10.)

Assuming the multiple items are of equal importance, effective writers may want to format each of them prominently to help busy readers to notice them all, even at the possible cost of obscuring the rest of the surrounding message. It can be a useful exercise to imagine a busy reader reading *only* the formatted content. Will the reader have learned all the essential information? If not, go back and revisit the questions we just raised.

Another approach some writers use in such a situation is to apply multiple formatting types in the same message. We typically advise against going down this perilous road. Not only does a lot of formatting dilute the impact of each formatted element, but multiple formatting types can create visual chaos that confuses readers. Consider the following email that one of us (Jessica) received from a taxi company a few years ago:

JESSICA, **IMPORTANT: READ THIS EMAIL IN ITS ENTIRETY**

Hello and thank you for remembering us. We can provide your one way service at the cash rate with a $25 Deposit payment below on the link where it says **"SELECT HERE"**
Once payment is processed we will send a payment confirmation email & you are **all confirmed & booked.**

Once PAID I will have your party (1) confirmed on my schedule for pickup

Friday, January 14, 20XX @10:00am
Pick up: [ADDRESS]
Drop off: [ADDRESS]
Rate: $79 one way
(Pick up & drop off only. Any store stops, extra cargo, wait time is an additional cost)
Contact ph no: 555-555-5555

PICK UP INSTRUCTIONS:

- We will contact you on the day of pick up with the contact phone number you provided.
- Once we are in the area we will reach out via phone call or text a few minutes prior to the pickup to be sure you are ready.
- If there are any questions or changes **PLEASE CALL 555-555-5555**

PAY NOW $25 DEPOSIT

1."SELECT HERE" Under the RED ARROW select "CLICK TO PAY NOW" button

2. You can Pay by Credit Card or PayPal account.

BALANCE OF $54.00 DUE AT TIME OF SERVICE IN *CASH ONLY!* DRIVER TIP NOT INCLUDED *Gratuity is customary & appreciated. Thank you!*

YOUR RECEIPT # / TRANSACTION ID # IS YOUR CONFIRMATION #
A final confirmation email will be sent once payment has cleared

Best Regards,

[SALESPERSON NAME]

Sales & Support Manager

Thank You for supporting our local Family Owned & Operated Business

This email uses it all: various font sizes, multiple font and highlighting colors (both shown here in shades of gray), bolding, all caps, underlining, italics, bullets, and more. The end result is colorful, comical, and confusing. What should the reader pay attention to? What information is most important? With so much going on here, readers will vary widely in what they think the writer intends to be most important.

When we've shown this email to students, some conclude that the most important information is the taxi pickup details. Others identify the phone number to call for help. Others identify the need to pay a $25 deposit. Still others say that the most important information is the balance that is owed at the time of pickup. Is the writer angry that the $54 balance hasn't been paid and that's why it's written in all caps? Or are they just underscoring that the $54 needs to be paid in the future? All these items being formatted, and formatted differently, leaves readers confused as to what is actually most important. A confused reader means that the writer has failed at clear communication.

The solution for the writer would have been to find the focal point hidden within that mess. On close reading, there appears to be one piece of information that is most important to the writer: The recipient must pay a $25 deposit to confirm their taxi reservation. Did you understand that after a quick skim? Jessica certainly didn't when she received it. Seeing the words "all confirmed & booked" bolded and underlined led her to believe that her reservation was, in fact, already confirmed and booked. It was only after a few reads that she realized she still needed to pay the deposit in order to confirm her ride. Had the email been formatted more effectively, it would have saved her time and effort. In this case, she did exert that time and effort and was able to pull out that key detail. Other readers very likely missed it, though. If so, the taxi company's poor formatting probably lost it some customers, and may have caused confused travelers to miss their flights.

The taxi email is the written equivalent of a peanut butter, ham, and Gorgonzola sandwich on banana bread: a combination of appealing ingredients that add up to an unpleasant, off-putting whole. Using too many types of formatting in a single message can leave readers unable to figure out what any of it means; they may be then less likely to read or understand the most important information. Formatting lots of items can be less effective than formatting none at all. But if you choose the appropriate ingredient and apply it judiciously, the result can guide your readers' attention exactly where you want it.

8

Fifth Principle: Tell Readers Why They Should Care

Most of us are not very good at imagining the world from someone else's perspective. In a whimsical but illustrative study, Stanford researcher Elizabeth Louise Newton divided test subjects into two groups, *tappers* and *listeners*. The tappers tapped out the rhythm of familiar songs such as "Happy Birthday" and "The Star-Spangled Banner"; the listeners tried to guess the songs being tapped. Then came the true test. Tappers were asked to imagine being listeners and to predict what fraction of the listeners would correctly identify the songs. Tappers predicted a success rate of 50%. In reality, listeners got it right just 2.5% of the time![1] Tappers were terrible at getting into the mindset of the listeners, and had no idea how terrible they were at it.

We writers tend to be similarly terrible at taking our readers' perspective. We think they devote more time to our messages than they do. We think that they find value in the same things that we do. In reality, as we've seen, writers and readers often have divergent goals. Readers routinely ignore messages that don't appear to meet their goals—and then our own goals go unfulfilled.

As writers, we can't necessarily change the topics we write about to make them more interesting or relevant to our readers. What we *can* do is train ourselves to understand our readers better so that we can communicate with them more effectively. We can strategically emphasize the aspects of our messages that we think our readers might care about most and articulate clearly why we believe they should care.

Even the most effective writing cannot guarantee success, but it can significantly increase the likelihood that busy readers read and engage with what we write.

THE RULES OF PERSONALLY RELEVANT WRITING

Rule 1: Emphasize What Readers Value ("So what?")

When readers regard a topic as personally relevant, they will exert more effort to understand it, read more deeply, and recall more content.[2] Researchers have experimentally confirmed what we've all noticed subjectively: People tend to devote more time and effort to things that affect them directly. In one study, the psychologist Richard Petty and his colleagues asked undergraduate students to read about a college policy under consideration, such as creating an exam requirement for graduation. When students were told that the college they currently attended was considering the policy, they read the policy more carefully and fully than when they were told a college in another state was considering it.[3]

A separate study conducted at the University of Notre Dame looked at the youth voter engagement organization Rock the Vote to explore how a sense of personal consequences can improve the success rate of a real message.[4] Rock the Vote, an organization created to recruit young voters at rock shows, emailed 19,990 people encouraging them to volunteer to register voters at live concerts. The emails went out in two versions.

The *Writer's Perspective* version included a subject line that reflected the writer's goal of recruiting new volunteers. The *Reader's Perspective* version included a subject line that focused instead on something that the recipient might value:

Writer's Perspective:
Subject: Volunteer with Rock the Vote
Reader's Perspective:
Subject: Want to attend free events?

The *Reader's Perspective* version also included a sentence in the body of the message reiterating, "You'll get to see the best shows for free and do important work at the same time!" Email list subscribers who received the *Reader's Perspective* version were nearly four times as likely to sign up to volunteer as those who received the *Writer's Perspective* version.

WRITER'S PERSPECTIVE

TO: [NAME]
FROM: Rock the Vote
SUBJECT: Volunteer with Rock the Vote

Dear [NAME],

There are big elections across the country in 2010. And here in Colorado, with your help, Rock the Vote is going to register young people to vote at concerts and festivals, bars and block parties, on campus and off. Will you join the Rock the Vote Street Team in your community or on your campus?

Click here to sign up to volunteer with Rock the Vote in Colorado.

Rock the Vote is committed to engaging young people in Colorado. This year we're focusing on people who have turned 18 since the 2008 election and those who have moved—they need to re-register at their new address! Be part of the movement to get young people registered to vote and back to the polls in 2010.

We already have a few great events planned, so click here to check out the events and sign up to volunteer.

I'm looking forward to working with you.

Sincerely,

[COORDINATOR NAME]
Colorado State Coordinator

READER'S PERSPECTIVE

TO: [NAME]
FROM: Rock the Vote
SUBJECT: Want to attend free events?

Dear [NAME],

There are big elections across the country in 2010. And here in Colorado, with your help, Rock the Vote is going to register young people to vote at concerts and festivals, bars and block parties, on campus and off. Will you join the Rock the Vote Street Team in your community or on your campus?

You'll get to see the best shows for free and do important work at the same time!

VOLUNTEER >

You'll get to see the best shows for free and do important work at the same time!

Click here to sign up to volunteer with Rock the Vote in Colorado.

Rock the Vote is committed to engaging young people in Colorado. This year we're focusing on people who have turned 18 since the 2008 election and those who have moved—they need to re-register at their new address! Be part of the movement to get young people registered to vote and back to the polls in 2010.

We already have a few great events planned, so click here to check out the events and sign up to volunteer.

I'm looking forward to working with you.

Sincerely,

[COORDINATOR NAME]
Colorado State Coordinator

In this example, appealing to readers' self-interest—a free concert sounds good!—helped Rock the Vote accomplish its goal of increasing volunteers. In this case, the organization was targeting young people, who are likely to be music lovers, but free concerts aren't the only thing readers care about. They may also be motivated to help others, to express their values, to conform to the behavior of others, or to just be seen as a good person.[5] In the same experiment, Rock the Vote tested additional messages that emphasized these other topics. None yielded as many volunteer sign-ups as the "free concert" message, but other types of readers in other contexts will inevitably respond differently. It is important to understand the perspective of your specific readers, and to test different messages, when possible.

The Rock the Vote study also highlights an important ethical consideration in appeals to the reader's personal desires and goals. Some recipients of the *Reader's Perspective* version may have opened the email because they were tempted by the prospect of free concert tickets, but had no interest in volunteering. These readers would have wasted their time reading a message that they were ultimately not interested in, and in doing so may have felt misled. At the same time, other recipients may have engaged with the message because of the appeal of free concert tickets but then discovered that—despite not anticipating it—they *were* interested in volunteering. These same readers might have ignored the *Writer's Perspective* message. Those readers would end up better off for having received the *Reader's Perspective* version, since it allowed them to discover an opportunity they valued that they would have otherwise missed.

Ultimately, the people who crafted the Rock the Vote emails, like all writers, had to balance the costs and benefits of emphasizing different information. Perhaps the cost of time for concert-loving readers who have no interest in ever volunteering is an acceptable price to pay for recruiting more volunteers. In other contexts, the risk of misleading readers or wasting their time may outweigh the benefits of using the approach reflected in the *Reader's Perspective*. If the reader-oriented message seems fundamentally deceptive, or if the reader is not sympathetic to the writer's goals, the communication can end up alienating its target audience in addition to wasting their time.

A good shorthand for writers who are working on practical communications is: "So what?" Try to picture the recipient of your message and consider what would make that person care about what you are saying. An additional factor to consider is not only why the reader should care but why the reader should care *now*—that is, the timeliness of the message. We'll talk more about this in chapter 10.

Even the simplest daily messages (text messages, work emails, Slack threads) are more effective if you write them with the recipient's perspective in mind.

Rule 2: Emphasize Which Readers Should Care ("Why me?")

Accurately predicting *what* ideas readers will care about is difficult, so another useful strategy is to target your message by emphasizing *which* readers should care. If a message seems generic and impersonal, readers may broadly presume that it is not relevant and ignore it. In that case, the specific readers for whom the message is relevant might miss out on valuable information.

Being explicit about your intended audience is especially

pertinent in mass communications that are difficult to target to specific populations. If the city government needs to notify residents that a local library will be closed for construction, this is relevant only for people who use that particular library—but city officials don't necessarily know who those people are. In such cases, emphasizing which readers a message is relevant for can help save readers time and increase the chance that the information reaches those who need it.

Think about what happens when a grocery item, say Soup XYZ, needs to be recalled due to safety concerns. Grocery stores that sold the recalled soup don't have a list of all the individuals who purchased it, but they *do* have websites and mailing lists and physical store locations where they can post notices. Then they face the question of how to make sure the correct recipients notice and care about the message.

When writing the recall notice, the stores could title it based on what their goal is from their perspective, alerting shoppers that a recall has been issued:

Writer's Perspective: *Notice: Important product safety recall information*

The *Writer's Perspective* could be relevant to everyone, but it is so generic that we predict it would get through to almost no one. A *Reader's Perspective* title would instead emphasize which readers the message is relevant for:

Reader's Perspective: *Notice: If you bought Soup XYZ in June, it has been recalled*

By tailoring the title toward those readers who should care about the message, the *Reader's Perspective* title likely increases the number of relevant readers who engage with it. It also helps readers for whom the message is irrelevant to know to skip it, making it both more effective and kinder to busy readers.

In everyday personal and business communications, often there is just one person at the other end. But we all run into the same issues of targeting as soon as the message expands to a group text, an office email list, a widely read Slack channel, and so on. In this case, there's another simple shorthand test to apply: "Why me?" Imagine the recipient looking at the message and asking, "Why me? Why did I receive this message?"

You probably know the experience of getting a mass email about a company outing you care nothing about or notifications about a distant acquaintance's vacation adventures. As long as the messages were clear up front about who they were aimed at, you probably ignored them and went about your day. If you wasted your time reading something irrelevant, though, you may have felt irritated, even cheated. To write effectively, bring that perspective to your own writing; be clear about who you expect will care and why they should care. Such targeting will make your messages more personal to the readers you are trying to reach and less disruptive to the ones you aren't.

9

Sixth Principle: Make Responding Easy

Sometimes the primary goal of our writing is to share ideas and make sure they are understood by the reader. Such writing comes in a wide variety of forms and levels of ambition. Your goal may be to make sure other parents at your school know about a PTA meeting later in the week, for instance, or to tell your coworkers about recent successes and challenges in your department. You might want to share family news, or make sure your neighbors know about a new policy affecting your neighborhood. Essays, articles, even entire books can fall into this category. Regardless of the scale, though, the end goal is fundamentally *informational*: You want the reader to pay attention to and engage with what you are saying.

Many types of common messages are response oriented, however. Not only do you want your readers to read and understand your message, you also want them to perform a concrete *action*. Here, too, the scope of the goal can vary enormously. Often your goal will be for the recipient to do something specific and focused, such as scheduling a meeting, responding to a request, applying for a program, signing up for a newsletter or webinar, attending school more often, or filling out an online form. But sometimes your ambitions may extend to inspiring readers to donate money, volunteer for a cause you care about, or campaign for a candidate in an upcoming election.

For action-oriented messages, you need your recipients to read and understand your message, but that is not enough. Even if the readers understand your request, and even if they engage with it enough to want to fulfill it, they may still fail to do so if it is too difficult or time-consuming. The fundamental limits of time and attention mean that many busy readers will decide that acting now is too costly. They will either postpone action, in which case they're likely to forget to return, or they may decide against acting entirely. This chapter focuses on how we increase the likelihood that readers will take the actions we request.

TL;DR: Make the request as easy as possible to comply with.

THE RULES OF EASY-RESPONSE WRITING

Rule 1: Simplify the Steps Required to Act

One of the most potent ways to increase the likelihood that people will act is to make the action happen without any effort on their part. That is, you can set up a default action that will take place automatically if they do nothing at all. For instance, many utilities and banks send paper bills to their customers each month. Paper is the default. Customers "choose" it passively if they do not bother to make a choice. They can also actively choose to switch to paperless (electronic) billing.

A prominent example of the power of defaults is in the context of retirement savings. Many employers in the US offer full-time salaried employees various retirement plan options. Standard enrollment processes require workers to *opt in*: They receive information about the retirement plans, and then have to take deliberate steps to enroll. However, studies consistently find that automatically enrolling workers into a plan, with an option to actively *opt out* instead, dramatically increases participation rates.[1] Opt-out messages have been effective in encouraging many other behaviors, too, including joining an organ donor registry,[2] getting flu shots,[3] and enrolling in electricity programs that use only renewable energy.[4]

When changing the default isn't possible, merely simplifying the process for taking action can dramatically increase the likelihood that readers act. One of the easiest ways to simplify the process is to reduce the number of steps required. In one study, we worked with the District of Columbia Public Schools in Washington, DC, to implement a text message update program for parents of 6,976 middle and high school students.[5] The program sent parents automated weekly updates informing them when their child missed class, failed to turn in an assignment, or had a low average course grade.

To receive updates, parents had to enroll in the program. All parents were first sent a text message informing them that the school district was rolling out this new program. They were then sent an invitation to enroll. Busy parents often do not follow through on such invitations, however. We therefore started testing ways to make it easier to sign up for the program, and tracked how different approaches affected enrollment.

The first group of parents received a text message inviting them to enroll by logging into the school district's parent portal and activating the service. At the time, that was the standard practice for inviting parents to enroll. Fewer than 1% of the parents contacted this way signed up. A different group of parents received a text message inviting them to enroll by simply replying "START" to the text itself, with no need to log in online separately. In this case, 11% of the parents signed up. Finally, a third group of parents were told via text message that they had been automatically enrolled in the program (that is, we had made enrolling in the service the default option), but that they could opt out at any point by responding "STOP." In this group, 95% of parents remained enrolled. And the service improved student academic success: When their parents were assigned to the opt-out group, students' grades increased and the number of courses they failed decreased.

Again, changing the default option proved to be the most powerful method of getting parents to sign up for weekly updates. Yet, simply allowing parents to enroll via a single text message, as opposed to requiring them to go through a separate sign-up process online, increased enrollment more than tenfold, from 1% to 11%.

As writers, we often do not control the steps we're asking people to take. Big decisions like changing the enrollment process for text updates (much less setting the default for organ donations or corporate retirement plans!) are often beyond our reach. But there are many small things we can do in the messages we send to make life easier for the readers by reducing the number of steps required for them to act. Take meeting scheduling, for instance. In an effort to be polite, many of us tend to ask open-ended questions like the following:

Want to talk next week?

This type of flexible request can easily turn into a series of back-and-forth emails trying to find a mutually agreeable time to meet. A more effective alternative is to suggest a meeting duration, day, and time organized in a way that's easy to understand and respond to, like the following:

Want to meet for 30 minutes next week? If so, how about one of these times (all ET):

- *Tuesday (3/13) at 10:30 am*
- *Wednesday (3/14) at 12:00 pm*
- *Thursday (3/15) at 3:00 pm*

Notice how this message also makes use of some of our earlier rules about clarity in order to preempt common scheduling questions and mix-ups. Do you mean this week or next week? (Next week, as indicated by the dates.) Are the times proposed my time zone or your time zone? (They are all clearly stated as ET.) This message saves all people involved from sending and receiving additional, unnecessary emails. It also increases the chance a meeting will be scheduled.

One study conducted by the vice chancellor's office at a major US university took this process a step further by giving readers the option of scheduling directly via Calendly, an appointment-scheduling app that integrates with online calendars. In a test, 115 university alumni leaders were sent an email requesting a meeting. After a brief introduction that provided context for the meeting request, the email ended with one of the following two asks:

Standard: *At a time that works with your schedule, would you have availability for a brief meeting via Zoom or phone? Please let me know if you have any questions, and I look forward to hearing from you to coordinate our meeting.*

Easier: *At a time that works with your schedule, would you have availability for a brief meeting via Zoom or phone? For your convenience, I am including a link directly to* ***my calendar*** *where you may select a time that works best for you.*

The *Easier* request offered readers the option of directly signing up for an available meeting time, whereas the *Standard* request required readers to reply with their availability. The office was able to secure meetings with 33% of those who received the *Easier* request, compared to just 17% of those who received the *Standard*. We should note a caveat, however: Some people have told us that they feel insulted when someone sends them a digital calendar link to schedule a meeting, especially if the other person is the one initiating the meeting request. Although this strategy was effective at the university where it was tested, it could come across as overly intrusive in other contexts.

You also need to be mindful of context in applying this strategy to other types of communications. If you are asking for a favor from a coworker, for instance, you wouldn't want to phrase it such that it feels like you are forcing them to say yes. If you are proposing meeting up with a friend, you would do well to be more specific than "Do you want to meet next week?" But it would sound quite presumptuous to say, "Let's meet at 6:30 on Tuesday at Restaurant ABC. I'll see you there unless I hear otherwise."

As with every other rule, the rule of easy-response writing requires understanding both your readers and their context.

Rule 2: Organize Key Information Needed for Action

Another way to increase the likelihood that readers will take action is to make all the information required to perform that action easily accessible. If possible, include all the essential details directly within the message, using the rules of clarity and design to make them readily noticeable to a busy reader. To illustrate, consider a very common type of personal and business communication: a series of email exchanges that unfold over many messages. When responding to a long, multi-email chain, writers will often reference earlier emails rather than summarize the entire exchange. The result is messages like this:

> *See the message below, sent on April 3, and let me know what you think.*

Referring back to earlier emails may save the writer time, but that approach often ends up requiring more time and effort from the reader. In the example above, it forces the reader to search through the email chain (possibly quite a long series of nested messages) to find the message sent on April 3. If the writer had simply restated the pertinent information from the April 3 message, that would make responding faster and easier for the reader.

Sometimes providing necessary information involves aggregating and paring down information that is already available elsewhere. In 2006, President George W. Bush signed legislation providing prescription drug benefits to people on Medicare. Recipients were given dozens of possible plans to choose from. Policymakers figured that more choices were better than fewer choices. They reasoned that since the choice of benefit plans was economically important, citizens would deliberate and select the best plan for themselves. To help recipients make an informed choice, the policymakers even created a website that generated personalized cost information, and they sent printed letters to recipients that included the eighty-four-character link to the website. This way, all recipients could go online, thoroughly research each plan option, and choose the one that best fit their needs. All they had to do was type in that link and navigate the site.

Government researchers recognized that navigating to and through the drug benefits website to learn about all the different plans required a great deal of time and effort. They wondered if organizing the key information in a simpler way would improve people's ability to choose the best plan for them. As a test, the researchers sent 5,873 Medicare recipients one of two letters. Half received the original letter referring them to the Medicare website (with the link spelled out), along with a booklet on how to use the site. The other half received a simplified letter containing the information they would have found on the website: personalized information on their current plan, a comparison to the lowest-cost plan, a recommended plan, and details on how much money the recipient could save by switching plans. Although the same information was freely available on the website, providing it directly in the letter—rather than asking recipients to go online to access it—almost doubled the number of recipients who switched plans, going from 17% to 28%. The simplified letter led to dramatic savings. If everyone in the study had received just the simplified letter the average person would have saved $100 on medications, *per year.*[6]

Providing busy readers with streamlined, well-organized information can also reduce the number of steps required to act. Government agencies increasingly encourage people to use online tools for tasks such as school enrollment, tax filing, and immigration applications. These communications typically begin by telling the reader something along the lines of:

> *Did you know you can file your immigration forms online at [government website]?*

Although providing the web link is helpful, readers hit a barrier as soon as they load the site. To get started they have to enter their username, something that people frequently forget or misplace. The message would be even more useful if readers were provided with the username required to access the website as well:

> *Did you know you can file your immigration forms online at [government website]?*
>
> *Your username is [name] and you can log in at [website].*

This kind of personalization isn't always feasible because of logistical and privacy constraints. But when it's possible, it can increase the likelihood that readers take the requested action. Personalization might also save the sender time and money if it reduces the volume of emails and phone calls the sender has to handle requesting these details.

In a less controversial way, almost all writers could be more conscientious in aggregating information and presenting helpful details to their recipients, rather than making them dig through email chains, previous text messages, or old documents that may have been filed away or discarded. As an effective writer, part of your job is to ensure your readers have all the necessary information in one accessible location. If readers have to seek out the information needed to act, they will be more likely to put it off and eventually forget the request entirely.

Rule 3: Minimize the Amount of Attention Required

The limits of the attention system in our brains make it difficult to follow through on tasks that require a lot of focus, particularly when we are busy. Minimizing the amount of focused attention required to act is therefore another effective way to increase the likelihood that readers will follow through on requests. This can be accomplished in many ways, including limiting the choices offered to the reader, constraining the response options, and clearly outlining the processes for responding.

Writers commonly offer their readers too many choices. Providing many options might seem kind and considerate, but what it actually does is impose an unintentional "attention tax" on the recipient. Studies confirm that when we have too many choices, we often put off making a decision until later (or never) because it's too hard to choose right now.[7] Limiting the number of options makes choosing easier and less depleting. President Obama expressed this strategy well when he told an interviewer: "You'll see I wear only gray or blue suits . . . I'm trying to pare down decisions. I don't want to make decisions about what I'm eating or wearing. Because I have too many other decisions to make."[8]

Minimizing the amount of attention required to act can have important pragmatic consequences. Returning to our earlier example of retirement savings: Employees who are offered retirement savings plans often have to make many decisions before they can enroll. They have to decide how much they want to contribute to the plan, for instance, and then choose how to allocate their savings across available funds and assets: bond funds, stock index funds, growth funds, and so on. These complicated, time-consuming decisions can deter many people from enrolling in the plans, even if they generally prefer to do so.

A study conducted at a large health services company examined whether simplifying this decision-making process could increase enrollment rates in retirement plans. Working with two different companies, a research team tested the impact of offering employees the option of enrolling in a retirement savings plan whose attributes were preselected by their employer, including a preset contribution rate and asset allocation. The researchers compared that alternative to the status quo process, which required employees to make an active choice among all available options if they wanted to enroll. Offering employees the option of a preselected plan increased enrollment rates by 10 to 20 percentage points.[9] Reducing the amount of attention required directly led to higher participation rates.

A related approach to minimizing the amount of focused attention required is to limit what is being asked of the reader. This technique applies in many familiar settings. Consider the following, quite typical workplace questions:

> **Broad:** *How was yesterday's senior staff meeting?*
> **Narrow:** *In yesterday's senior staff meeting, did we decide whether we're submitting a bid for the project?*

Which of these would be easier to respond to? The open-ended nature of the *Broad* question makes it more time-consuming to respond to. Presented with the *Broad* question, the reader has to synthesize their thoughts about the entire meeting and summarize them into a message. Meanwhile, the *Narrow* question focuses the reader on one specific dimension of the meeting: whether the team decided to submit a bid. The *Narrow* question can be answered with a simple and undemanding yes/no response. Note that, in this case, the shorter message is not the easier message for the reader; it may be shorter, but it is also more open-ended. All else being equal, the writer may get more fruitful feedback from the *Broad* question—but only if the reader replies, which is less likely, given how much attention it requires.

Productivity software can help writers insert these kinds of directed questions into emails, converting them into minipolls that allow just a few, predefined response options. This constraint can discipline writers to narrow down their questions, and can also make it easier for readers to quickly and easily answer the questions. With practice, though, writers can also train themselves to keep their action requests limited and focused.

Messages that require more focused attention don't just waste the reader's time. They can also cause misunderstandings and mistakes, which can have huge implications. The confusion caused by the notorious "butterfly ballots" in Palm Beach County, Florida, actually changed the outcome of the 2000 US presidential election.[10]

Voters who carefully examined this ballot would understand that they needed to follow the arrow associated with their preferred candidate's name to the black dot in between the left and right pages and punch a hole to cast their vote. But busy or distracted voters could easily misunderstand this. Reading the left page first, they would see the two major party candidates listed first (George W. Bush) and second (Al Gore). If they were going quickly, they might thus conclude that punching the

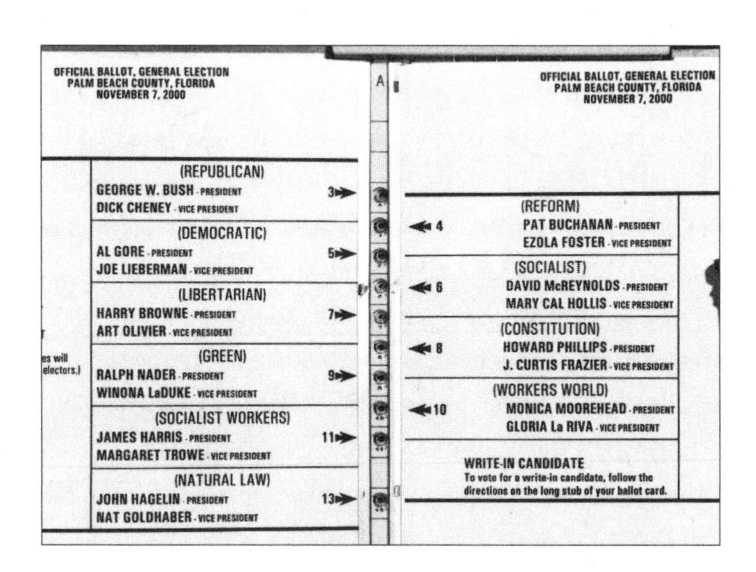

OFFICIAL BALLOT, GENERAL ELECTION
PALM BEACH COUNTY, FLORIDA
NOVEMBER 7, 2000

(REPUBLICAN)
GEORGE W. BUSH - PRESIDENT
DICK CHENEY - VICE PRESIDENT
3

(DEMOCRATIC)
AL GORE - PRESIDENT
JOE LIEBERMAN - VICE PRESIDENT
5

(LIBERTARIAN)
HARRY BROWNE - PRESIDENT
ART OLIVIER - VICE PRESIDENT
7

(GREEN)
RALPH NADER - PRESIDENT
WINONA LaDUKE - VICE PRESIDENT
9

(SOCIALIST WORKERS)
JAMES HARRIS - PRESIDENT
MARGARET TROWE - VICE PRESIDENT
11

(NATURAL LAW)
JOHN HAGELIN - PRESIDENT
NAT GOLDHABER - VICE PRESIDENT
13

es will
electors.)

A

OFFICIAL BALLOT, GENERAL ELECTION
PALM BEACH COUNTY, FLORIDA
NOVEMBER 7, 2000

4
(REFORM)
PAT BUCHANAN - PRESIDENT
EZOLA FOSTER - VICE PRESIDENT

6
(SOCIALIST)
DAVID McREYNOLDS - PRESIDENT
MARY CAL HOLLIS - VICE PRESIDENT

8
(CONSTITUTION)
HOWARD PHILLIPS - PRESIDENT
J. CURTIS FRAZIER - VICE PRESIDENT

10
(WORKERS WORLD)
MONICA MOOREHEAD - PRESIDENT
GLORIA La RIVA - VICE PRESIDENT

WRITE-IN CANDIDATE
To vote for a write-in candidate, follow the directions on the long stub of your ballot card.

first hole between the pages would indicate a vote for Bush (correct) and that punching the second hole would indicate a vote for Gore (incorrect). Punching the second hole instead indicates a vote for Pat Buchanan of the Reform Party.

Analyses suggest that this butterfly ballot resulted in more than two thousand people who intended to vote for Gore mistakenly casting their votes for Buchanan. Gore lost Florida by 537 total votes, less than the number of votes intended for him but mistakenly cast for someone else. The outcome in Florida, in turn, decided the entire presidential election and put Bush in the White House.[11] It is not hyperbole to say that the outcome of the 2000 US presidential election would have been different if the Palm Beach County ballot had been written to reduce the amount of focused attention required of readers.

One final way for you to minimize the attention required from your readers is to clearly and simply outline the steps or process required to act. Just as readers may be deterred from acting if they have to search for the necessary information about what to do, readers may also be deterred if they don't understand the steps required—*how to do it.*

In one study, researchers worked with the US Internal Revenue Service (IRS) to test different styles of communications about California's Earned Income Tax Credit, often abbreviated as EITC.[12] The EITC is a tax credit for eligible low-income and moderate-income workers. It can substantially reduce the amount of taxes they owe or increase the amount of money they get back each year. But in order to receive the EITC, eligible workers must both file their taxes *and* claim the credit each year. In a typical year, around 20% of people who are eligible for the EITC don't claim it.[13]

The researchers tested two versions of a written notification informing low-income individuals that they may be eligible for the EITC. The *simplified* version employed many of the principles in this book and, critically, included a clear explanation of the action steps being requested of the reader:

> **WHAT YOU NEED TO DO**:
>
> *Complete the Earned Income Credit Worksheet on Page 3.*
>
> ***If the worksheet confirms that you are eligible for the credit***
> *Sign and date the attached worksheet, and mail it to us in the enclosed envelope.*
>
> ***If the worksheet indicates that you are not eligible for the credit***
> *Please do not return the worksheet to us.*

In contrast, the *complex original* version included a list of six bullet points that offered instructions for filling out an enclosed worksheet, and a footnote that instructed, "*Note: Return the [EITC] Worksheet to us* ***only*** *if you determine you may qualify for the [EITC].*"[14] The more complex notice yielded a response rate that was a substantial 27% lower than the response rate for the simple notice.

As with all the rules we outline, this approach also requires a balance. Note that we call for both clear and *simple* outlines of the process. If the explanation is overly complex or complicated, it may actually deter readers from acting. In the same EITC study, the researchers documented this effect. They tested two variants of the EITC eligibility worksheet: a version that included two primary eligibility criteria and another version that listed seven. The more complex worksheet contained more relevant details, but it decreased response by 17%.

For low-income people, simplifying the application process for the earned income tax credit makes a big difference in their quality of life. In the case of the 2000 vote, failure to pay attention to ease of response changed the outcome of an election. Most readers of this book are probably not going to end up in situations where democracy hangs in the balance based on how effectively they write. But the principles and rules of effective writing that can spur a reader to action are useful and potentially even life-changing in all kinds of settings.

PART THREE

Putting the Principles to Work

10

Tools, Tips, and FAQs

The six principles outlined in this book are overarching guidelines. They establish the *what* of effective writing—the fundamental techniques you need to communicate effectively with busy readers. But none of us communicate in a vacuum. There are endless complicating factors that intrude the moment we send our messages out into the world. Dealing with that reality requires a set of practical methods to address the *how* of effective writing—the tools and tactics that will help you put the six principles into practice.

As teachers, researchers, advisers, and public speakers we get questions about the *how* of effective writing all the time. For instance, people ask, should we cut out all extraneous content in an effort to make a message as concise as possible, or should we start with a "gratuitous" warm introductory sentence to appeal to our reader? Is it better to send one message containing three requests or three messages with one request each? How do I choose the right medium for a message? How do I optimize the timing? How do I convey the urgency of a message without seeming too pushy or too vague? How can I adapt my tone so that it balances the core elements of effective writing with the specifics of my personal voice and my distinctive audience?

There are no simple universal answers to these types of questions, since every situation is different. In the end, it is up to you to know your readers and to make the judgment calls about how to write to them. That said, we offer insights to help you, as an effective writer, make the best decision for your specific context. We have structured this chapter around the most common questions we've encountered as educators, as public speakers, and as writers ourselves. Think of this as the FAQ (frequently asked questions) section of the book: It is a knowledge base for effective writers seeking to refine and adapt their skills.

WHAT IF I HAVE A LOT TO SAY?

For practical communicators, writing less can often seem like an impossible challenge. How do we say everything we want while still being concise? How long is too long? Striking the right balance is hard, but two things may help.

First, *edit for conciseness.* It's difficult to write concisely on the first try. After writing an initial draft, pause for a moment and then take another pass, looking closely for anything that can be said in fewer words. These days, you can use software to help you. Apps like Grammarly and newer versions of Microsoft Word can highlight sentences and phrases that could be made more concise. If you still struggle with cutting your own words, you may find it easier to write a brand-new, more concise second draft from scratch, rather than spend time editing the first. However you do it, editing for conciseness is an important part of the practical writing process.

Second, *take a cold, hard look at what is truly necessary to include* in your message. Is everything in your message essential to your goal as a writer? Can anything be punted to a later communication? If all pieces of information in your message are equally important to communicate right now, it raises a separate question about how to handle communications with multiple purposes. We discuss that in a bit. But a lot of the time, our early drafts suffer from "mission creep," where the purpose shifts and broadens beyond the initial writing goal. If your writing seems unwieldy, refocus on the original primary goals, or even reconsider whether those goals were already too broad and ambitious.

Ultimately, writers must balance their desire to communicate everything relevant with the understanding that the more they add, the less readers will read. This may be an acceptable trade-off in some cases, especially when reaching more readers is not the paramount goal. Writers of legal terms and conditions are less concerned with maximizing reading than with satisfying disclosure requirements. For them, completeness may trump conciseness, and legal compliance may trump ease of reading.

One strategy we often use in our own work is to place valuable but noncritical content in an attachment, appendix, link, or below the signature line of a message. We refer to the additional content in the main writing, but we push it out of the main text so it doesn't pull attention away from the primary message. This approach can help bridge the writer's desire for more information with the reader's need for less.

Bottom line: In keeping with our first principle, writers should aim to use the fewest number of words, ideas, and requests necessary to achieve their goals, and no fewer.

(HOW) DO THE PRINCIPLES OF EFFECTIVE WRITING APPLY TO LONGER-FORMAT WRITING?

The overall principles of effective writing apply regardless of the scope of your writing. Sure, if you're trying to write the next Pulitzer Prize–winning novel, these principles will only take you so far. But longer-form writing—especially professional styles of long-form writing, such as essays, project summaries, annual reports, and review articles—should be easy to read, navigate, and understand, regardless of its length.

In some ways, making your writing easy on the reader is even more important in longer formats than in shorter ones. If your employer expects you to write a twenty-page briefing, it needs to be twenty pages! But it can still be written using familiar words, straightforward sentences, concise paragraphs, streamlined formatting, and a small number of well-formulated ideas.

In long-form writing, it is also especially important to know your goals. This is a piece of advice we had to constantly remind ourselves about as we wrote the book you are reading. The longer the message, the more challenging it can be to stay focused on why you are writing and what outcome you hope to achieve. Keeping your writing goals clear and top of mind can help you decide what information stays and what goes.

WHAT IF I NEED TO COMMUNICATE MULTIPLE PIECES OF EQUALLY IMPORTANT INFORMATION?

Even in fairly short messages, writers sometimes must include multiple pieces of important information. To pick one common example: Healthcare clinics traditionally reach out to new patients (1) to ask for insurance information; (2) to provide check-in instructions; and (3) to remind them of their first appointment time. All three pieces of information are equally critical to communicate now; none can be withheld for a later date.

In that situation, writers can either communicate all the information in a single message or send multiple messages, each with one purpose or piece of information. There's no hard-and-fast rule on which option is better. In one of our surveys of working professionals, 72% of the respondents said that they prefer to receive one message containing three pieces of information rather than three separate messages, each with one piece of information.[1]

Context matters, though. Different audiences may have different expectations, reading styles, and personal preferences. Readers' preferences also don't necessarily align with writers' goals. The easiest way to meet people's needs is by directly asking what they want. Much as many companies now ask people whether they prefer to receive information via text or email instead of paper, writers could also ask their readers whether they prefer to receive bundled or separated requests. But this isn't always possible, so there are a few questions we recommend writers ask themselves to help them navigate through this situation:

Are all pieces of information related to the same event, behavior, or requested action?

If so, it may make sense to combine them into a single message. That is what healthcare clinics usually do. Overall, it can be less effective (and more annoying) for a medical office to send patients three separate emails—one requesting insurance information, another with check-in instructions, and another with appointment details—than to send a single email covering all of them. The details all directly relate to the same upcoming doctor's visit, so it makes sense to deal with them together. But if the various parts of your message do not fit together neatly like that, you are probably better off communicating them separately.

If you are asking the reader to take multiple actions, are they all likely to be completed at the same time? Are some harder or more time-consuming to complete than others?

Imagine a family member emailing to ask what time the reader expects to arrive at the family holiday dinner . . . and to request their thoughts on appropriate holiday gifts for other family members . . . and also to ask for help finding an old family cookie recipe. The question about arrival time could be answered quickly on the reader's phone while on a bus or waiting in line. The gift suggestion might require a little thought. Finding the family cookie recipe could involve some serious digging.

Responding to multiple requests in a single message can be difficult if they require different amounts of effort. Some readers may respond quickly to the easy requests and subsequently forget the harder ones. Other readers may hold off on responding until they can answer everything at the same time, which means waiting until a moment when they have time to tackle the hardest request and remembering to do it. Often that magical moment of abundant free time never actually arrives. In this case, it may be better to separate the easy requests from the harder requests and communicate them in different messages.

HOW CAN I GET READERS TO ENGAGE WITH MESSAGES CONTAINING A LOT OF INFORMATION?

Regardless of whether multiple pieces of information are bundled or separated, previewing how information is being delivered helps busy readers. A message containing multiple pieces of information can state this explicitly at the top:

> *I've included three points below: (1) an update on the status of your home renovation; (2) a request for your approval for new light fixtures; and (3) a request to schedule a time to talk.*

Similarly, if the writer of this message had chosen to split each piece of information into a separate message, that, too, could have been previewed:

> *I am writing to provide an update on the status of your home renovation. I will follow up shortly with an additional message that will ask for your approval for new light fixtures and to schedule a time to talk.*

Using introductory text to tell readers what the rest of the text is about is called "signposting." Signposting is not the core content being written about, but rather a road map for the rest of the writing. Although it typically adds words, it can be helpful for making longer messages or messages with multiple pieces of information easier to navigate.

Another strategy, as we described above, is to place lower-priority (but still necessary) information in secondary locations. You can include the information but move it out of the main message, using phrases like "See the attachment for more on this topic." Or you can separate the information by placing it in an appendix or link, or by pasting it at the end of the message below your sign-off.

WHAT IF MULTIPLE COMMUNICATIONS ARE REQUIRED (REMINDERS, REPEATED ACTIONS, MULTIPLE STEPS)?

Writers often need to communicate with the same readers repeatedly. Sometimes they need to remind readers about an upcoming event, such as a scheduled medical appointment, or to take an action they have so far failed to do, such as responding to a survey. Other times, writers prompt readers to take an action they've taken repeatedly in the past, such as paying their monthly credit card bills or filing their annual income taxes.

Communicating repeatedly with the same audience is hard, in part because people can have divergent responses to multiple contacts. Some readers may grow accustomed to repeated messages, especially if they appear similar. People can become desensitized and start to pay less attention to each subsequent message. On the other hand, some research suggests that readers find it easier to process information they have seen before, and they may actually like things better the more they see them. In this case, people may be *more* likely to pay attention to similar subsequent messages.

These contradictory responses can make life confusing for writers. But there are two key factors that can help: the frequency and consistency of repeated communications. Paying attention to these factors will help you strike a good, effective balance.

Frequency: How many messages are too many? Sending too many messages can risk causing your readers to tune out all your messages. Readers may delete or ignore all future communications from a sender who sends too many messages. They may also unsubscribe from a list or may even block certain senders if that is an option. So you want to minimize non-essential communications.

At the same time, cutting the number of communications too much risks losing your readers entirely. Repeated messaging is often necessary because people tend to forget and procrastinate—especially when they're busy. For instance, researchers have found that sending patients reminders about upcoming health-care appointments can reduce the number of no-shows.[2] Regular reminder messages have also been found to increase a number of other behaviors, like saving money[3] and paying child support.[4]

When deciding on the right message frequency, writers need to balance these benefits of timely reminders with the risk of sending so many messages that readers tune them out. As part of another "get out the vote" study, researchers mailed registered voters up to ten messages encouraging them to vote in an upcoming election.[5] The first five mailed messages each incrementally increased voter turnout over and above the prior mailer. But the last five messages had no further effect.

In extreme cases, sending too many messages backfires and becomes worse than sending fewer of them. In a study conducted in Kenya, a team of researchers set out to find ways to increase adherence to an HIV treatment regimen among local HIV/AIDS patients. A group of 431 patients were randomly assigned to receive daily or weekly text message reminders to stay on top of their regimen.[6] Over a forty-eight-week period, 32% more patients who received weekly reminders achieved target adherence rates than patients who received no reminders. But the adherence of patients who received daily reminders did not improve; their adherence rates were similar to those of patients who did not receive any reminders at all. The study authors speculate that daily reminders may have felt intrusive, or that the messages came so often that the patients stopped devoting attention to them.

As with much of our other guidance, the modified "less is more" principle applies here: Send just as many communications as you crucially need (and as often as you crucially need), but no more. Empathize with your readers and consider what the messages look like from their point of view. Imagine if a utility company decided to cut its communications down to a single notice sent once a year reminding customers to pay their bills on the first of every month. Most people (ourselves included) would likely forget to pay their bill on time occasionally—a yearly reminder is not often enough to provide useful guidance. Now imagine if the utility decided to send *daily* reminders about paying your monthly bill. You would probably start to ignore the notices or find a way to stop them, and would then again occasionally forget to pay the bill.

These extreme examples are useful for helping you fine-tune your own strategy. Think about what would maximize your own engagement if you were in the reader's position.

Consistency: When communicating repeatedly with the same readers, writers often wonder whether each message should be the same (in content, messenger, and format) for consistency or different for variety. The answer depends on the type of information being communicated, but there is some useful guidance to draw on.

In one study conducted with a large provider of open-access online courses, we examined whether it was more effective to vary the subject lines of weekly emails or to keep them the same. We found that varying the subject lines increased the likelihood that students opened the course emails.[7] Because these particular emails were purely informational, containing reminders and updates about the courses and program, they were relatively low value. When the subject line was constant week after week, students likely learned that the messages could safely be ignored. Essentially, they used the subject line as a rule of thumb for determining whether the email would be useful, and therefore whether they should engage with it. In contrast, when the subject line changed each week, the students had to open the message to determine how valuable it might be. That might have wasted some of their time, but it might also have exposed them to relevant information they would otherwise have missed.

For more action-oriented messages that readers find useful, keeping the subject line, format, or overall packaging consistent can help readers more quickly recognize that the message is worth engaging with. Notice how credit card companies send highly consistent messages—whether by email or physical mail—each time a bill is due? They typically use the exact same style, format, and envelopes (if they're mailed) or subject lines and senders (if they're emailed) every month.

In contrast, political campaigns know that their readers may not find their fundraising messages particularly valuable, so they routinely vary the email subject lines or physical mailed envelopes. Each one might look quite different even though they all have the same goal: to solicit a donation.

Once you are clear about your goals and understand how your messages are likely to be received by your readers, you can judge whether consistency or variety will be the more effective communication strategy.

CAN I USE TECHNICAL LANGUAGE WHILE STILL APPLYING THE SIX PRINCIPLES?

Writers communicate to a broad range of readers across many different contexts. The language we use often differs depending on the intended readers. Statisticians communicating to other statisticians may be able to use mathematical language in their communications. These mathematical terms would be familiar to their readers and could help make the communication clearer and more concise. Other readers, however, might find the Greek letters and formulas impenetrable.

So, yes, technical language can be used in effective writing, but writers should do so with caution. When you edit for conciseness, you should also review your language to make sure it matches the needs and expectations of your readers. Knowing your audience is the best way to ensure that your language matches their needs and expectations.

WHAT IF I NEED TO ADDRESS MANY DIFFERENT AUDIENCES WITH THE SAME MESSAGE?

The principles of effective writing are relevant regardless of whether a communication is intended for one individual or for millions of people. But the practical application of these principles can vary depending on how broad and diverse the audience is. Managers, politicians, medical professionals, group leaders, university deans, people doing publicity or public outreach, and others often need to appeal to a wide range of readers at the same time in both language and content.

In terms of the complexity of language, this often means using the words that will be most familiar to the broadest cross section of your readers. If a manager leading a team that includes engineers, marketers, and designers sent a message to the full team using technical language familiar only to the engineers, it might be inaccessible and even alienating to the rest of the team.

Appealing to a diverse set of readers who may have differing interests and needs often requires adding more words. A city council member may need to address multiple constituencies (and their respective concerns) in a single update. Doing so technically goes against the "less is more" principle, but sometimes more is necessary to achieve your ultimate writing goals.

WHO SHOULD BE THE MESSENGER?

Who sends and signs a message can powerfully affect how readers respond to it. That is, the same information delivered by different people may be received differently. Much of the time, writers are simply communicating on their own behalf, especially in personal or one-to-one messages. In these cases, no choice is needed; the writer acts as their own messenger. But in many contexts, such as organizational updates, sales pitches, and fundraising appeals, communications could come from a number of different messengers.

Ever notice how political campaigns send similar fundraising messages repeatedly, each with a different sender? Different senders catch the attention of different readers, so campaigns do this with the hope of capturing more attention and more donations. Campaigns might choose a messenger who is familiar to and trusted among specific audiences. Similarly, advertisers or corporations may mix up the genders and ethnicities of their messengers to appeal to different audiences.

When you have a choice of messenger, there are several attributes to pay attention to. Credibility is particularly important: Readers are more likely to respond to and act upon messages that come from sources they trust and admire. In one study, researchers varied the messenger of letters aimed at encouraging low-income Californians to check their eligibility for and claim the Earned Income Tax Credit.[8] Half the recipients got a letter from the Franchise Tax Board, the California state agency that administers and collects taxes. The other half received a letter from Golden State Opportunity, a California-based nonprofit organization. Both letters directed recipients to a website where they could check their eligibility for the tax credit. People who received the letter from the Franchise Tax Board were three times as likely as those who received the Golden State Opportunity letter to visit the website, probably because the Franchise Tax Board is more well-known and seen as more credible.

Expert, familiar, and trusted messengers also tend to be more effective at getting people to take action across a wide range of activities, from encouraging charitable donations[9] to informing people about the risk of smoking cigarettes.[10]

Given the complexities of finding the right messengers, it may be tempting to conjure up a fictional expert to be a message's sender. Beyond the obvious ethical issues of deceiving readers, a fake expert can also cause backlash once the deception is uncovered. LendEDU, a student finance company, experienced this when it concocted a person named "Drew Cloud." He was presented as an expert in student loans and gave interviews online. He was quoted in leading news sources, often advocating for refinancing student debt, which LendEDU could profit from. In 2018, *The Chronicle of Higher Education* uncovered that he was invented by LendEDU. The deception continues to follow the company.[11]

WHEN SHOULD COMMUNICATIONS BE SENT?

We're often asked during workshops when messages should be sent to maximize the likelihood that readers will respond. There's no one answer here, either. Messages sent in the morning are not necessarily better than ones sent in the evening, nor are Mondays reliably better than Thursdays. That said, there are a few useful guiding principles about timing.

Send messages when your readers are most likely to have time and motivation to read and respond.

Optimal timing can vary a lot from group to group, and over time. Imagine being a teacher and needing to communicate with a busy parent about an assignment their child must complete for tomorrow. Sending a message in the morning would mean the parent would have to use their limited attention to remember that information many hours later, when their child comes home from school. If the message were sent in the afternoon, the parent might be able to discuss it with their child soon thereafter, reducing the chance they would forget or get distracted. Then again, if most of the parents work in the afternoon and are too busy to read email then, the morning would be better, despite the burden of needing to remember all day.

Now consider another situation: A worker must ask a busy colleague one single, time-sensitive question. Sending the message at the beginning of the business day would give the colleague an entire day to come up with an answer, whereas sending it at the end of the day would increase the chance that they forget to respond by the time they return to work the following morning. But this assumes the colleague reads the message sent in the morning. If they deal with their emails last in, first out, the morning email may end up buried beneath the other messages sent throughout the day.

Ultimately, understanding your specific readers is the best way to know when the "right" time is to send communications.

Send action-oriented messages close to the time when that action needs to be taken.

Communications that request an action should be sent as close as possible to when the action needs to be taken while still leaving enough time for the reader to act on it. Sending a reminder on September 15 to file income taxes due April 15 is unlikely to be effective; by the time April rolls around, most people will have long since forgotten the reminder. At the same time, sending a reminder on April 14 to file income taxes due April 15 is also likely ineffective, but this time since most people need more than one day to complete and file their taxes. You want your readers to feel an appropriate level of urgency—focused but not panicked—when they receive your message.

EMAIL, CHAT, TEXT, MAIL: WHAT IS THE RIGHT MEDIUM FOR MY MESSAGE?

These days, our options for delivering communications can feel limitless, and at times overwhelming. Different methods of communication each have their own strengths and weaknesses. Some organizations explicitly set standards for how they expect employees to communicate. People also have their own, varied preferences: Some like email for updates and text messages for scheduling; others like the exact opposite. When possible, we recommend asking people which method they prefer for different types of information. But when that's not possible, we recommend using the medium that best fits the message's purpose and the needs of readers, considering the length and format of the message and your reader's typical behavior.[12]

Despite (or perhaps because of) the rise in digital communications over recent decades, paper-based communications are still often effective, especially for readers who are inundated with digital messages via email and text message. Since they can physically persist, they can also serve as physical reminders when a requested action is time-consuming, must be performed later, or requires multiple, staggered steps. One of our studies found that postcards were nearly twice as effective as emails at increasing college students' enrollment in CalFresh, California's food stamp program.[13] We weren't able to study exactly why postcards were so much more effective, but there are two likely reasons. First, they may capture more attention because they are less common than emails. Second, they may stick around in the reader's physical world, repeatedly directing attention to the food stamp program until the student has the time and motivation to enroll.

Matching your communication method to your target audience is also important. Some audiences may have limited access to technology or may be less comfortable with it, making paper-based communications more appropriate. Digital communications can also impose burdens on certain populations, especially if direct engagement or interaction is required. In one study, parents in historically disadvantaged communities in Greece were invited to seek information on free dental care for their children through four types of communication.[14] Parents were eighteen times as likely to use a prepaid postcard to request information as to use email or phone to request the information. This disparity was, in part, because parents lacked confidence and self-efficacy in in-person (phone or email) interactions. At the same time, some audiences are better reached via email or text message, especially if mailing addresses are unavailable or likely to be out-of-date. For many readers, an email or text is simpler and more convenient than a print message.

It's important to note that the norms for each communication method vary not just by context but also over time. Such changing patterns can influence their effectiveness. Studies conducted in 2006 found that a single text message reminding people to vote increased turnout by 4 percentage points.[15] In 2010, we conducted research showing that a single text message increased turnout by about 1 percentage point.[16] By 2017, text messages were found to have almost no effect on turnout.[17] Apparently, text messaging became a less effective way to deliver important information to voters.

The change in the way people have responded to text messages may have a lot to do with novelty and volume. In 2006, texting was relatively new for most people, and few organizations sent text messages. When people received a message, they therefore paid attention and read it closely. Today, it's common practice for organizations to send texts; many of us even receive spam texts. As a result, most people probably pay a lot less attention to unsolicited text messages now than they did in 2006. And as we have underscored throughout this book: Engaging with the message is the first result of effective communication. As digital communication evolves, we would expect similar patterns to arise for whatever becomes the next commonplace form of messaging.

	STRENGTHS	**WEAKNESSES**
Chat platforms (e.g., Slack, Microsoft Teams)	Good for real-time collaboration and urgent, time-sensitive requests (if people stay accessible). Good for organizing messages across topic channels.	Can easily be forgotten if they're not responded to immediately, making them less well-suited for situations where an immediate response isn't required or possible. Can generate a large volume of communications and notifications, which can cause readers to disengage.

	STRENGTHS	WEAKNESSES
Text messages	Reach people nearly instantaneously, making them ideal for messages that can be delivered exactly when the requested action can be performed, if readers pay attention to their text messages.	Tend to disappear from attention after they've been read, making them not ideal for future-oriented actions or actions with multiple steps over time.
Emails	Good for documenting communication. Useful for delivering more-detailed information than can fit in a text message, especially including attachments. Relatively inexpensive for delivering mass communications. Good for directing people to online sources via links.	Have hit saturation, increasing the risk that any single message will get lost or read too late, no matter how important it is.
Paper mail	Can become a "social artifact" that sticks around even after it's been delivered; can be talked about and physically shared. Can be useful for not losing track of actions to be implemented in the future, or actions requiring multiple steps over time.	Slower and more costly to deliver than digital types of messaging.

HOW DO I WRITE FOR SOCIAL MEDIA?

Although research on the topic is still evolving, we propose something that may sound radical: Social media writing should adhere to the same principles as other forms of practical writing. We've already noted that people are more likely to engage with social media posts that are more readable.[18] Social media writing can similarly benefit from applying the other five principles. Even in short, modern formats, effective writing is still effective writing.

The *goals* of writers may be different in social media, however. Posts on Facebook, Instagram, TikTok, Twitter, and the like tend to be about more than merely efficiently transferring information to readers. Writers often want their posts to be amusing and worthy of sharing. This can require extra complexity and nuance, even while working within tightly constrained word counts. Social media posts therefore need to balance the principles of effective communication with the more personal, informal style and goals of the medium.

HOW SHOULD I USE HYPERLINKS IN DIGITAL MESSAGES?

One of the strengths of digital communications is that it makes it easy to connect readers to other online sources. Most writing software automatically underlines and changes the color of hyperlinks to help readers spot where to click for more information or to take an action. Similar to other kinds of formatting, hyperlinks can help capture readers' attention: Some eye-tracking research shows that readers who are skimming spend more time on hyperlinks than on nonhyperlinked words.[19] But if hyperlinks are not the most important information in a message, they can crowd out other information, much as other types of formatting can.

One large school district we worked with sent an email with several paragraphs that looked like this:

> For more information, and a list of qualifying items, please see the Department of Revenue's Taxpayer Information Publication on the 2021 Disaster Preparedness Sales Tax Holiday. As a reminder, we list prioritized severe weather (hurricane) days on our 2021–22 school calendar.

We find the overloaded format difficult to read. The reader's attention is naturally drawn to the differently colored hyperlinks. This may leave readers confused about what's most important. Since hyperlinks don't seem to be the most important information here, it would be helpful to minimize the number of words the links highlight:

> For more information, and a list of qualifying items, please see the Department of Revenue's Taxpayer Information Publication on the 2021 Disaster Preparedness Sales Tax Holiday. As a reminder, we list prioritized severe weather (hurricane) days on our 2021–22 school calendar.

Streamlining is especially important for readers who use audio reading tools to understand their emails. Such tools typically make note of which words are associated with links. Linking the fewest words possible while also ensuring that the hyperlinked words convey some meaning can help everyone, but especially the visually impaired and others who rely on audio reading tools.

IS IT APPROPRIATE TO USE SARCASM, HUMOR, OR EMOJIS?

Humor and sarcasm are risky because people can easily misunderstand them in their written form. When reading, people don't have access to facial cues, intonation, and other subtleties that convey the true intent of the communication. Even when writers think their sarcasm is obvious, readers are often left confused. In one telling study, people were asked to write sarcastic messages and then predict what fraction of readers would recognize that they were being sarcastic. The writers predicted 78% success. In reality, readers were no better than fifty-fifty at detecting sarcasm in writing.[20]

Emojis can lead to similarly unintended and unanticipated confusion, especially across varied age groups.[21] Smiley faces tend to be interpreted as sincere positivity among older readers, whereas younger readers often interpret them as patronizing or passive-aggressive.[22] The meanings of different emojis also change over time, making it even more complicated to know when and how to use them appropriately. If you know the norms and expectations of your audience, emojis can help convey emotion or humor.

As the variety of emojis has expanded, they are increasingly used to express serious ideas as well. For instance, a judge ruled in February 2023 that some emojis have important financial and legal consequences because they are unambiguous in their meaning (at least for now). The judge wrote that 🚀, 📈, and 💰 "objectively mean one thing: a financial return on investment."[23] It remains to be seen whether emojis continue to evolve to take on serious connotations and meanings. For now, though, writers should be cautious and clear when using emojis in important writing, given their wide range of possible interpretations.

Writers often have a goal of being seen as funny or less serious by their readers. If that's your goal, go for it (and good luck 😉). But you will probably need to signal more strongly than you think necessary that you are trying to be funny.[24] Explaining that you're being sarcastic may take away from the humor, but it can also alleviate misunderstanding and confusion.

WHEN SHOULD I USE PICTURES INSTEAD OF WORDS?

A picture is worth a thousand words, as the cliché goes—but those thousand words may not be the ones you're trying to convey. If translating words into an image can save readers time while serving our goals as writers, then using pictures instead can make sense. If the picture increases complexity, confuses, or distracts the reader, though, including it is probably a mistake.

Sometimes images are included for purely aesthetic reasons. This may be a useful strategy for increasing reader engagement or reader perceptions of professionalism, as long as the images don't distract readers, or unnecessarily tax their attention. If you want to include a graphical element for visual appeal, you might also want to consider charts, graphs, tables, or other design elements that might convey your core message more efficiently, as discussed in chapter 6.

11

Our Words, Our Selves

As much as we wish that all writers were viewed equally, that's not the way of the world we live in. Readers have expectations about how certain types of people *should* communicate. They have biases and assumptions about how certain types of people *do* communicate. They are quick to make inferences about communicators based on how a message is written, from the choice of words to the syntax to the overall structure and tone. A one-line email may be perceived as rude coming from certain senders yet entirely acceptable coming from others.

Stereotypes based on gender, race, ethnicity, and social status intrude into everything we do. Writing is not immune. The same stereotypes spill over into how readers perceive messages from various groups, especially groups outside their own. Communications from women, racial or ethnic minorities, or people in low-status positions may be regarded differently (usually less favorably) than communications from men, White people, or people in high-status positions. The way we are perceived can affect how effective our messages are, adding another level of complexity to all the principles we cover in this book.

In one anecdotal but all-too-familiar story, two professional editors—one male, one female—switched email signatures (and hence their perceived genders) for a week when communicating with clients.[1] The female editor found clients were more receptive and took her more seriously when she was using her male colleague's signature. Meanwhile, when the male editor used his female colleague's signature, he found clients questioning more of his suggestions than he was accustomed to, and behaving in a more condescending manner.

Randomized experiments conducted in the United States have repeatedly shown bias against writers who are perceived to be women or minorities. For instance, people are less likely to respond to emails from people they believe to be Black than from people they believe to be White. This has been found to be true among the general public,[2] professors at universities,[3] state legislators,[4] and public service providers, such as school districts, local libraries, and county clerks.[5] In a similar vein, university faculty have been found to rate male applicants for a junior-level research position as more competent and hirable than female applicants.[6]

A writer's identity also tends to influence the language they use, perhaps because writers are aware that the way they are perceived can influence the way their messages are received by readers. When lower-status writers write to higher-status readers, they tend to write longer messages containing relatively few direct requests, whereas higher-status writers tend to do the opposite.[7] Compared to men, women are more likely to write using signals of warmth such as exclamation points,[8] apologies,[9] and qualifying statements like "I think" and "I feel."[10] But when women compensate by "emailing like men," women writers report, they are often perceived as "too cold" or "too aggressive."[11] It's a catch-22 faced by writers from many stereotyped groups.

SHAPE YOUR IDENTITY AS A WRITER

We have limited control over our external identities, and we cannot alone change the fundamentals of how society perceives us. All we can do is be conscious of how our words (and, thus, ourselves) may be perceived and how that perception may affect our goals as writers. The need for added attentiveness is unfair, since the burden falls disproportionately on members of disadvantaged groups. It also requires a precarious balancing act. We do not want to perpetuate negative stereotypes by accommodating them. At the same time, we want to help writers of all types and backgrounds to write effectively—and, realistically, doing so requires writing with an awareness of how our messages may be received by others based on how others perceive us.

Before composing any message, writers have to decide on their overall style and tone. Often there are context-specific norms you can turn to for guidance. A fundraising letter or an office memo about the company's financial results doesn't leave much room for personal adjustments. But in everyday communications we often face a wide range of options. Should you send a formal black-and-white letter or an informal colorfully designed postcard? Should you greet readers with, "Hi, friend!" or "To whom it may concern"? These decisions will depend on your professional (or nonprofessional) circumstances, but also on your perceived identities. Readers routinely look at the style of a communication, in terms of both language and design, to infer the writer's likability, credibility, relatability, and goals.

As one example, some research has found that readers are more likely to respond to government communications written in relatively formal language, in part because formality acts as a signal of credibility in the public-sector context.[12] Another study found that politicians who use more informal language on social media are seen as less credible because the style goes against how people expect politicians to sound.[13] People are similarly less likely to trust unfamiliar consumer brands that use informal communication on social media, because of norms about how companies should sound—although, like all norms, these appear to be evolving.[14] Such considerations can become even more complicated when personal identity is added to the equation, as when someone with a lower-status personal identity is communicating from a higher-status professional position.

As a general rule, a formal communication style works better when that is what readers expect. In some contexts, though, an informal style may be more appropriate and effective; a formal style might even seem inappropriate. Writing an overly stiff email to a close colleague or friend, for instance, is likely to come across as strange or rude. But writing an overly informal email to a person in a position of power may *also* come across as rude. In both cases, readers may be deterred from responding because of what the communication style signals.

Like formality versus informality, the trade-off between warmth and conciseness is a familiar one for many writers. We often include content that is unconnected to our primary goals but that is instead intended to make our messages more friendly and polite—traits that are valued in both professional and personal contexts. Think about all the emails that start, "Hope this finds you well!" Such greetings may seem superfluous from the standpoint of "less is more," but they are an important part of human interaction. Cutting all extraneous content from a message risks coming across as aggressive or rude, which could decrease the chance that readers engage with it.

Striking the right balance between precision and personality is especially consequential for writers who are women, racial and ethnic minorities, or of lower social or professional status. Power, status, race, gender, and other stereotyped identities can affect how readers expect people to write, and especially the warmth they are expected to convey. Many such writers may find that including "more," in the form of warm, personable, and polite language, helps serve their goals, even if it results in slightly less concise messages. That said, the "less is more" principle remains as relevant as ever, just in a form that reflects the world we are writing for. Including a single warm, personalized sentence at the start of a message may help engage your reader and buffer against harmful expectations. Including two paragraphs of personal preamble may backfire, lose your readers, and even harm how you are perceived.

Understanding the expectations and norms of readers is

critical for choosing an appropriate and effective communication style. But sometimes we have to take control of those norms, or refuse to give in to readers' expectations. A writer may be perceived as low-status because of race, gender, or other aspects of their identity, despite writing from a nominally high-status government job. In this case, it is not the writer's job to accommodate the possibility that the reader might expect excessive warmth or formality. Social norms and expectations have changed greatly over the past few decades, partly through the actions of people (including writers) who refused to bend to social and cultural expectations.

We are keenly aware that we, the authors of this book, are ourselves writing from a position of privilege. We work at a high-status university, and we often receive the benefit of the doubt in our writing as a result. But the principles of effective writing are not just our subjective, personal observations. They are communications strategies that have been widely studied, analyzed, and tested. They are rooted in universals of human nature: the mind's limited attention and focus, the rules of thumb it uses, the behaviors of busy people, and the ways that we give and receive information through written messages.

Although we cannot know your specific setting, dynamics, and context, ultimately the principles of effective writing apply regardless of your particular identities and situation. The principles help you optimize within your constraints. All else being equal, fewer words are better than more words. Requiring less effort to respond is better than requiring more effort. Above all, making it easier for readers is better than making it harder. But because writers are perceived differently based on their identities, the practical application of these principles may look different for different writers in different settings. Being aware of readers' stereotypes, inequitable as they may be, is crucial to writing effectively.

APPLY THE TRUTH TEST

There is one aspect of identity that we have not addressed yet, because it is so deeply implicit in everything that has come before: honesty. The principles of effective writing are all based on the assumption that you, the writer, genuinely want to be understood. We have taken for granted that the writer's stated goal is the same as the writer's actual goal. In the real world, though, that assumption is not always correct.

In certain settings, a writer's goal is not to be read and understood but rather the exact opposite. Some writers aim to obfuscate, obscure, and hide information they must disclose but would rather not. Empirical evidence shows that firms write more obtusely when disclosing to investors CEO compensation packages and other critical financial matters,[15] and scientists write more complexly when their research is fraudulent.[16] Sometimes writers are paid to spread misleading ideas and outright lies on behalf of corporations, politicians, governments, advocacy groups, and other organizations. Such writers are distressingly common on social media, though propaganda and disinformation are hardly modern inventions.

We cannot offer guidance for writers who are specifically aiming to not be clear. That runs counter to the principles of our book, as well as counter to the more general principles of ethical communication. We can offer some guidance for readers, however: Be cautious and attentive when you come across a message that seems deliberately complicated. Most of the time it will probably just indicate that the writer does not understand how to communicate effectively. But sometimes, unclear writing belies one of the most important truths that a message can contain: that the writer has something to hide.

12

Now What?

The big goal of this book is to make the principles of effective writing an automatic part of your regular writing process. Anything that requires a lot of conscious attention is draining; we all naturally want to avoid or defer difficult tasks. The more you practice effective writing, though, the easier it becomes. Think of it like learning to sing, type, or drive. At first, those tasks seem intensely demanding, requiring your full attention. Eventually they become so familiar that you can do other tasks on top of them, such as answering a phone call while cruising down the highway or listening to music while typing out a report.

No question, learning to write effectively requires an up-front investment—but the investment pays off in multiple ways. Throughout this book, we've focused on the benefits that effective writing has for the reader, but we've noted many examples of benefits to the writer as well. It's worth reiterating this point: Effective writing is not a form of altruism for the reader, although it certainly does make the reader's life easier. It is really a way for writers to clarify and distill their own goals, and to increase the likelihood that those goals are achieved.

Miscommunication stemming from ineffective writing can harm friendships. It can derail your career, especially if you are in a profession in which you deal with the public or you regularly interact with your colleagues through writing. In extreme cases, as with the 2000 US presidential election, it can literally change the course of history. And it robs you of one of the most wonderful, magical powers you have as a human: the ability to transmit ideas from your head into someone else's.

Once you tap into the power of effective communication, its benefits operate at all scales. Yes, it is useful for getting your coworkers to respond to an office questionnaire or for scheduling dinner with a friend. But, as we have seen, it is also useful for helping students stay out of debt or for making sure that sick patients show up to their doctor's appointment. Effective writing can be vibrant—full of humor, empathy, emotion, style, and perspective. On the grandest scale, it can be applied to the most important things in life: to advance the pursuit of justice and prosperity, to guide parents through difficult situations, to offer meaningful messages of solace and support to people who are grieving.

Although the principles of goal-oriented writing are timeless, as ancient as the process of writing itself, the application of those principles is always evolving. For one thing, effective writing is influenced by the medium in which it is transmitted. Twenty years ago, social media was a new and exciting medium. Thirty years ago, the same was true for text messaging. Forty years ago, it was true for email. Partly, too, effective writing is influenced by changes in culture and social norms. Attitudes toward race, gender, and other aspects of personal identity have changed almost as rapidly as the changes in technology. As technology and society continue to evolve, writing is sure to follow.

We are not technologists, and we certainly are not clairvoyant, so we won't attempt to predict what everyday practical writing will look like in another forty years. But it is safe to say that with every technological change there will come new forms of communication, and that each one will bring new norms, opportunities, and challenges. We can also confidently predict that readers will continue to have too little time and too little attention. So there will continue to be a pressing need for effective writing that is easier for readers. As we were writing this book, large-language-model AI chatbots like ChatGPT exploded into the mainstream. These tools were trained to analyze and mimic the ways real humans write. They are already becoming remarkably sophisticated at organizing text coherently, in ways that can convince readers that the large-language-model AI is writing with conscious intent.

Such chatbots could be extremely helpful in assisting writers—for instance, by generating first drafts from bullets, polishing final drafts, or offering initial suggestions to get writers past the agony of starting with a blank screen. But as we've shown throughout this book, effective writing must be informed by how people *read* and by all of the ever-shifting contexts and expectations that influence the reading process. Large-language-model chatbots aren't yet trained to write with this additional insight (maybe one day!). For now, writers are still left to their own devices to translate their goals into effective writing for busy readers.

We opened this book by asserting that if busy readers move on from our writing without understanding it, it's our fault. We can sit back and hope readers pay close attention to everything we write, or we can accept that it's our job as writers to meet busy readers where they are, as they are. Doing so requires revisiting our writing with a reader's perspective. If you take nothing else away from this book, we hope you'll at least remember to ask yourself, "How can I make this easier for the reader?" every time you write. We promise that doing so will help both you and your readers. And in some ways, maybe small but maybe big, it will help make the world a kinder, more accessible, more productive, and more connected place.

Writing for Busy Readers

SIX PRINCIPLES

1 Less Is More

1. Use fewer words
2. Include fewer ideas
3. Make fewer requests

2 Make Reading Easy

1. Use short and common words
2. Write straightforward sentences
3. Write shorter sentences

3 Design for Easy Navigation

1. Make key information immediately visible
2. Separate distinct ideas
3. Place related ideas together
4. Order ideas by priority
5. Include headings
6. Consider using visuals

4 Use Enough Formatting but No More

1. Match formatting to readers' expectations
2. Highlight, **bold**, or underline the most important ideas
3. Limit your formatting

5 Tell Readers Why They Should Care

1. Emphasize what readers value ("So what?")
2. Emphasize which readers should care ("Why me?")

6 Make Responding Easy

1. Simplify the steps required to act
2. Organize key information needed for action
3. Minimize the amount of attention required

For a printable version of this checklist, go to www.writingforbusyreaders.com

Appendix

Words and Alternatives

You might enjoy the list of common phrases and the more succinct alternatives we recommend on our website, www.writingforbusyreaders.com.

Acknowledgments

Though "less is more" is a central tenet of writing effectively, more is better when it comes to developing a book. Our mentors, colleagues, students, friends, and family have continuously helped us along the way. For this we are immensely grateful, and the science of writing for busy readers is immeasurably better.

Thank you for your patience, encouragement, ideas, and inspiration to the people listed here—and to the many others who have shared their thoughts and time. All wisdom in this book is thanks to you. All errors are our own.

Family and friends: Sara Dadkhah, Caroline Rogers, Fletcher Rogers, Ami Parekh, Andy Kucer, Brian Kucer, Chris Koegel, Emily Bailard, Kirk Allen, Matt Wessler, Nat Bessey, Sharon Wong, Ted Satterthwaite, and Wil Harkey.

Mentors, colleagues, and collaborators: Allison Brooks, Angela Duckworth, Arielle Keller, Bobette Gorden, Carly Robinson, Carmen Nobel, Cass Sunstein, Chris Mann, Danny Oppenheimer, Dave Markowitz, Dave Nussbaum, David Nickerson, Dolly Chugh, Elizabeth Linos, Evan Nesterak, Hedy Chang, Hillary Shulman, Hunter Gehlbach, Jeff Seglin, Julia Minson, Katy Milkman, Lauren Keane, Leslie John, Max Bazerman, Mike Norton, Nancy Gibbs, Nick Epley, Robert Cialdini, Ros Atkins, Sendhil Mullainathan, Sharad Goel, Sidney D'Mello, Taylor Woods-Gauthier, Zak Tormala, and all our incredible students and partner organizations.

The phenomenal professionals who helped develop vague ideas into this actionable text: Abigail Koons, Alexis Burgess, Celeste Fine, Corey Powell, Harsh Vardhan Sahni, John Maas, and Kelly Yun.

Finally, to the team at Dutton: Grace Layer, Stephen Morrow, Tiffany Estreicher, and Alice Dalrymple. Thank you for your commitment to this project and for your patience with the process.

Notes

INTRODUCTION

1. Bobby Allyn, "They Ignored or Deleted the Email from Airbnb. It Was a $15,000 Mistake," npr.org, December 12, 2020, https://www.npr.org/2020/12/12/945871818/they-ignored-or-deleted-the-email-from-airbnb-it-was-a-15-000-mistake.
2. Michael Chui, James Manyika, Jacques Bughin, Richard Dobbs, Charles Roxburgh, Hugo Sarrazin, Geoffrey Sands, and Magdalena Westergren, *The Social Economy: Unlocking Value and Productivity through Social Technologies* (n.p.: McKinsey Global Institute, 2012).
3. In the US, ballot initiatives allow citizens of some states to vote directly on new laws or constitutional amendments.
4. Shauna Reilly and Sean Richey, "Ballot question readability and roll-off: The impact of language complexity," *Political Research Quarterly* 64, no. 1 (2011): 59–67.

CHAPTER ONE: GET INSIDE YOUR READER'S HEAD

1. "Why Is Everyone So Busy?" *Economist*, December 20, 2014, https://www.economist.com/christmas-specials/2014/12/20/why-is-everyone-so-busy.
2. Alina Tugend, "Too Busy to Notice You're Too Busy," *New York Times*, March 31, 2007, https://www.nytimes.com/2007/03/31/business/31shortcuts.html.
3. Kira M. Newman, "Why You Never Seem to Have Enough Time," *Washington Post*, March 25, 2019, https://www.washingtonpost.com/lifestyle/2019/03/25/why-you-never-seem-have-enough-time/.
4. Patrick Van Kessel, "How Americans Feel about the Satisfactions and Stresses of Modern Life," Pew Research Center, February 5, 2020, https://www.pewresearch.org/fact-tank/2020/02/05/how-americans-feel-about-the-satisfactions-and-stresses-of-modern-life/.
5. Survey conducted with students in an executive education course, February 2021. N = 160.
6. George A. Miller, "The magical number seven, plus or minus two: Some limits on our capacity for processing information," *Psychological Review* 63, no. 2 (1956): 81.
7. Jon Hamilton, "Multitasking in the Car: Just Like Drunken Driving," npr.org, October 16, 2008, https://www.npr.org/2008/10/16/95702512/multitasking-in-the-car-just-like-drunken-driving?storyId=95702512.
8. Our definition of "attention" is broader than what is typical in academic research. Specifically, we use "attention" to mean a mental activity that can be channeled in a discrete moment to notice, direct, and focus. Some of the components of mental activity we include in our definition are working memory, focused attention, orienting, and executive function. For a review of how scholars think about attention and research on the various types of attention, see Steven E. Petersen and Michael I. Posner, "The attention system of the human brain: 20 years after," *Annual Review of Neuroscience* 35 (2012): 73.

9. L. Payne and R. Sekuler, "The importance of ignoring: Alpha oscillations protect selectivity," *Current Directions in Psychological Science* 23, no. 3 (2014): 171–77.
10. Jeremy M. Wolfe and Todd S. Horowitz, "Five factors that guide attention in visual search," *Nature Human Behaviour* 1, no. 3 (2017): 1–8, https://www.nature.com/articles/s41562-017-0058.
11. Https://www.ikon-images.com/stock-photo-busy-iconic-london-scene-illustration-image00023061.html.
12. Benjamin R. Stephens and Martin S. Banks, "Contrast discrimination in human infants," *Journal of Experimental Psychology: Human Perception and Performance* 13, no. 4 (1987): 558.
13. Wolf M. Harmening and Hermann Wagner, "From optics to attention: Visual perception in barn owls," *Journal of Comparative Physiology A* 197, no. 11 (2011): 1031–42.
14. Naotsugu Tsuchiya and Christof Koch, "Continuous flash suppression reduces negative afterimages," *Nature Neuroscience* 8, no. 8 (2005): 1096–101; Raymond M. Klein, "Inhibition of return," *Trends in Cognitive Sciences* 4, no. 4 (2000): 138–47; Daniel J. Simons and Christopher F. Chabris, "Gorillas in our midst: Sustained inattentional blindness for dynamic events," *Perception* 28, no. 9 (1999): 1059–74; Heather Berlin and Christof A. Koch, "Defense Mechanisms: Neuroscience Meets Psychoanalysis," *Scientific American*, April 1, 2009, https://www.scientificamerican.com/article/neuroscience-meets-psychoanalysis.
15. A. MacKay-Brandt, "Focused attention," *Encyclopedia of Clinical Neuropsychology*, eds. J. S. Kreutzer, J. DeLuca, and B. Caplan (New York: Springer, 2011): 1066–67.
16. Simons and Chabris, "Gorillas in our midst."
17. Brandon J. Schmeichel, Kathleen D. Vohs, and Roy F. Baumeister, "Intellectual performance and ego depletion: Role of the self in logical reasoning and other information processing," cited in *Self-Regulation and Self-Control*, by Roy F. Baumeister (Abingdon, UK: Routledge, 2018), 310–39.

18. William D. S. Killgore, "Effects of sleep deprivation on cognition," *Progress in Brain Research* 185 (2010): 105–29.
19. Filip Skala and Erika Zemková, "Effects of acute fatigue on cognitive performance in team sport players: Does it change the way they perform? A scoping review," *Applied Sciences* 12, no. 3 (2022): 1736.
20. Caitlin Mills, Julie Gregg, Robert Bixler, and Sidney K. D'Mello, "Eye-mind reader: An intelligent reading interface that promotes long-term comprehension by detecting and responding to mind wandering," *Human–Computer Interaction* 36, no. 4 (2021): 306–32; Shi Feng, Sidney D'Mello, and Arthur C. Graesser, "Mind wandering while reading easy and difficult texts," *Psychonomic Bulletin & Review* 20, no. 3 (2013): 586–92; D. M. Bunce, E. A. Flens, and K. Y. Neiles, "How long can students pay attention in class? A study of student attention decline using clickers," *Journal of Chemical Education* 87, no. 12 (2010): 1438–43.
21. Gloria Mark, Victor M. Gonzalez, and Justin Harris, "No task left behind? Examining the nature of fragmented work," in *Proceedings of the SIGCHI Conference on Human Factors in Computing Systems* (New York: Association for Computing Machinery, 2005), 321–30; Jennifer Robison, "Too Many Interruptions at Work?" *Gallup Business Journal*, June 8, 2006.
22. Bob Sullivan and Hugh Thompson, "Brain, Interrupted," *New York Times*, May 3, 2013, https://www.nytimes.com/2013/05/05/opinion/sunday/a-focus-on-distraction.html.
23. Publilius Syrus, *The Moral Sayings of Publius Syrus, a Roman Slave*, trans. D. Lyman (Cleveland: L. E. Barnard, 1856).
24. There is some evidence that the contemporary environment is making us better at dividing our focused attention between two tasks at the same time. But still, doing two (or more) things at the same time decreases our ability to do either as well as if we focused entirely on one thing at a time. For a thoughtful review, meditation, and guide on this topic, see Cal Newport's *Deep Work*.
25. Kevin Collins, "Why You Shouldn't Multitask and What You Can Do Instead," *Forbes*, July 15, 2021, https://www.forbes.com/sites

/forbestechcouncil/2021/07/15/why-you-shouldnt-multitask-and-what-you-can-do-instead/?sh=4f2afebdd01b.

26. Online survey conducted on MTurk, February 2022. N = 1,808.
27. We use the Stroop task to illustrate the challenge of managing attention when faced with two cognitive tasks, though we note that this task is more commonly used by attention researchers to illustrate the difficulty of directing attention selectively. It's a nice illustration of both cognitive challenges.
28. Stephanie Enz, Amanda C. G. Hall, and Kathryn Keirn Williams, "The myth of multitasking and what it means for future pharmacists," *American Journal of Pharmaceutical Education* 85, no. 10 (2021).
29. "Distracted Driving," National Highway Traffic Safety Administration, n.d., https://www.nhtsa.gov/risky-driving/distracted-driving.
30. Les Masterson, "Distracted Driving Survey 2021: Drivers Confess to Bad Behavior," insurance.com, August 8, 2021, https://www.insurance.com/auto-insurance/distracted-driving.

CHAPTER TWO: THINK LIKE A BUSY READER

1. Online survey conducted on MTurk, February 2022. N = 1,808.
2. Jessica Lasky-Fink and Todd Rogers, "Signals of value drive engagement with multi-round information interventions," *PLOS ONE* 17, no. 10 (2022): e0276072.
3. Katherine L. Milkman, Todd Rogers, and Max H. Bazerman, "Highbrow films gather dust: Time-inconsistent preferences and online DVD rentals," *Management Science* 55, no. 6 (2009): 1047–59.
4. Matthew Healey and Robyn LeBoeuf, "How Incentives Help Us Do Hard Things," n.d., https://sjdm.org/presentations/2020-Poster-Healey-Patrick-Difficulty-Task-Goals~.pdf; also, Susan C. Wilkinson, Will Reader, and Stephen J. Payne, "Adaptive browsing: Sensitivity to time pressure and task difficulty," *International Journal of Human-Computer Studies* 70, no. 1 (2012): 14–25.
5. Zohar Rusou, Moty Amar, and Shahar Ayal, "The psychology of task management: The smaller tasks trap," *Judgment and Decision Making* 15, no. 4 (2020): 586.

6. Online survey conducted on MTurk, February 2022. N = 452.
7. Online survey conducted on MTurk, February 2022. N = 450.
8. Samuel M. McClure, Keith M. Ericson, David I. Laibson, George Loewenstein, and Jonathan D. Cohen, "Time discounting for primary rewards," *Journal of Neuroscience* 27, no. 21 (2007): 5796–804; Samuel M. McClure, David I. Laibson, George Loewenstein, and Jonathan D. Cohen, "Separate neural systems value immediate and delayed monetary rewards," *Science* 306, no. 5695 (2004): 503–7.
9. For rats, see John Bascom Wolfe, "The effect of delayed reward upon learning in the white rat," *Journal of Comparative Psychology* 17, no. 1 (1934): 1. For birds, see G. W. Ainslie, "Impulse control in pigeons," *Journal of the Experimental Analysis of Behavior* 21, no. 3 (1974): 485–89; Howard Rachlin and Leonard Green, "Commitment, choice and self-control," *Journal of the Experimental Analysis of Behavior* 17, no. 1 (1972): 15–22. For schoolchildren, see Levon Melikian, "Preference for delayed reinforcement: An experimental study among Palestinian Arab refugee children," *Journal of Social Psychology* 50, no. 1 (1959): 81–86; Joan Grusec and Walter Mischel, "Model's characteristics as determinants of social learning," *Journal of Personality and Social Psychology* 4, no. 2 (1966): 211; Richard T. Walls and Tennie S. Smith, "Development of preference for delayed reinforcement in disadvantaged children," *Journal of Educational Psychology* 61, no. 2 (1970): 118. For chimpanzees, see Roger T. Kelleher, "Conditioned reinforcement in chimpanzees," *Journal of Comparative and Physiological Psychology* 50, no. 6 (1957): 571.
10. An executive education session in December 2022. Survey was administered with more than approximately 150 attendees.
11. K. Rayner and M. Castelhano, "Eye movements," *Scholarpedia* 2, no. 10 (2007): 3649.
12. Online survey conducted on MTurk, February 2022. N = 903.
13. Jukka Hyönä and Robert F. Lorch, "Effects of topic headings on text processing: Evidence from adult readers' eye fixation patterns," *Learning and Instruction* 14, no. 2 (2004): 131–52; Guy M. Whipple

and Josephine N. Curtis, "Preliminary investigation of skimming in reading," *Journal of Educational Psychology* 8, no. 6 (1917): 333.

14. Kara Pernice, "Text Scanning Patterns: Eyetracking Evidence," Nielsen Norman Group, August, 25, 2019, nngroup.com/articles/text-scanning-patterns-eyetracking.

CHAPTER THREE: KNOW YOUR GOALS

1. Adam Grant (@AdamMGrant), Twitter post, July 24, 2022, 10:10 a.m., https://twitter.com/adammgrant/status/1551208238581948416?lang=en.

CHAPTER FOUR: FIRST PRINCIPLE: LESS IS MORE

1. Marc Brysbaert, "How many words do we read per minute? A review and meta-analysis of reading rate," *Journal of Memory and Language* 109 (2019): 104047.
2. "Section: Blaise Pascal" in *The Yale Book of Quotations*, Fred R. Shapiro, ed., (New Haven: Yale University Press, 2006), 583.
3. G. S. Adams, B. A. Converse, A. H. Hales, and L. E. Klotz, "People systematically overlook subtractive changes," *Nature* 592, no. 7853 (2021): 258–61.
4. Katelyn Stenger, Clara Na, and Leidy Klotz, "Less is more? In patents, design transformations that add occur more often than those that subtract," in *Design Computing and Cognition'20*, ed. John S. Gero (Cham, Switzerland: Springer, 2022), 283–95; Leidy Klotz, *Subtract: The Untapped Science of Less* (New York: Flatiron Books, 2021).
5. Survey conducted during a training of professionals who work at a large nonprofit organization, December 2022. N = 166.
6. Online survey conducted with 12,230 school board members, August 2020. The experiment included three experimental conditions. Only two (N = 7,002) are reported here. Sample excludes emails that bounced back.
7. Online survey conducted on MTurk, February 2021. N = 493.

8. Noah D. Forrin, Caitlin Mills, Sidney K. D'Mello, Evan F. Risko, Daniel Smilek, and Paul Seli, "TL;DR: Longer sections of text increase rates of unintentional mind-wandering," *Journal of Experimental Education* 89, no. 2 (2021): 278–90.
9. Arthur Quiller-Couch, *On the Art of Writing*, vol. 10 (Cambridge, UK: Cambridge University Press, 1916).
10. "Her Time," *Time*, September 14, 2017, https://time.com/4941028/her-time-nancy-gibbs-editor/.
11. We have tested short versus long messages in four field experiments, using both email and text messages. In subsequent online studies, we then showed online survey participants the actual messages from the field experiments and asked them to predict whether the short or long message would be more effective at getting recipients to take the requested action. In each case, the majority of survey participants predicted that the longer message would be more effective—often the vast majority of participants made this incorrect prediction.
12. William Strunk Jr. and E. B. White, *The Elements of Style (Illustrated)* (New York: Penguin, 2007).
13. Study conducted with the Journalist's Resource, August 2021. N = 50,244.
14. Sinan Aral, Erik Brynjolfsson, and Marshall W. Van Alstyne, "Harnessing the digital lens to measure and manage information work," November 16, 2010, SSRN, https://ssrn.com/abstract=1709943.
15. When we showed the two messages side by side to forty-one professionals enrolled in an executive education program in January 2023, 59% thought the *Wordy* version "coherently flows better from one sentence to the next" compared to the *Concise* version.
16. T. M. Andrews, R. Kline, Y. Krupnikov, and J. B. Ryan, "Too many ways to help: How to promote climate change mitigation behaviors," *Journal of Environmental Psychology* 81 (2022): 101806.
17. Lester R. Lusher, Winnie Yang, and Scott E. Carrell, "Congestion on the Information Superhighway: Does Economics Have a Work-

ing Papers Problem?" National Bureau of Economic Research, Working Paper No. 29153, August 2021.

CHAPTER FIVE: SECOND PRINCIPLE: MAKE READING EASY

1. William H. DuBay, "The Principles of Readability," Impact Information, 2004, https://files.eric.ed.gov/fulltext/ED490073.pdf.
2. Christopher R. Trudeau, "The public speaks: An empirical study of legal communication," *Scribes Journal of Legal Writing* 14 (2011): 121.
3. Matthew S. Schwartz, "When Not Reading the Fine Print Can Cost Your Soul," npr.org, March 8, 2019, https://www.npr.org/2019/03/08/701417140/when-not-reading-the-fine-print-can-cost-your-soul.
4. Catharine Smith, "7,500 Online Shoppers Accidentally Sold Their Souls to GameStation," *HuffPost*, May 25, 2011, https://www.huffpost.com/entry/gamestation-grabs-souls-o_n_541549. Accessed March 18, 2023.
5. Ruth Parker, "Health literacy: A challenge for American patients and their health care providers," *Health Promotion International* 15, no. 4 (2000): 277–83.
6. Joseph Kimble, "Writing for dollars, writing to please," *Scribes Journal of Legal Writing* 6 (1996): 1.
7. Jill Diane Wright, "The effect of reduced readability text materials on comprehension and biology achievement," *Science Education* 66 (1982): 3–13.
8. Ethan Pancer, Vincent Chandler, Maxwell Poole, and Theodore J. Noseworthy, "How readability shapes social media engagement," *Journal of Consumer Psychology* 29, no. 2 (2019): 262–70.
9. Bin Fang, Qiang Ye, Deniz Kucukusta, and Rob Law, "Analysis of the perceived value of online tourism reviews: Influence of readability and reviewer characteristics," *Tourism Management* 52 (2016): 498–506.
10. David M. Markowitz and Hillary C. Shulman, "The predictive utility of word familiarity for online engagements and funding,"

Proceedings of the National Academy of Sciences 118, no. 18 (2021): e2026045118; David M. Markowitz, "Instrumental goal activation increases online petition support across languages," *Journal of Personality and Social Psychology* 124, no. 6 (2023): 1133–145.

11. Alan M. Kershner, "Speed of reading in an adult population under differential conditions," *Journal of Applied Psychology* 48, no. 1 (1964): 25; DuBay, "The Principles of Readability"; Kristopher Kopp, Sidney D'Mello, and Caitlin Mills, "Influencing the occurrence of mind wandering while reading," *Consciousness and Cognition* 34 (2015): 52–62.
12. Shi Feng, Sidney D'Mello, and Arthur C. Graesser, "Mind wandering while reading easy and difficult texts," *Psychonomic Bulletin & Review* 20, no. 3 (2013): 586–92.
13. Michael K. Paasche-Orlow, Holly A. Taylor, and Frederick L. Brancati, "Readability standards for informed-consent forms as compared with actual readability," *New England Journal of Medicine* 348, no. 8 (2003): 721–26.
14. Shauna Reilly and Sean Richey, "Ballot question readability and roll-off: The impact of language complexity," *Political Research Quarterly* 64, no. 1 (2011): 59–67; Jason C. Coronel, Olivia M. Bullock, Hillary C. Shulman, Matthew D. Sweitzer, Robert M. Bond, and Shannon Poulsen, "Eye movements predict large-scale voting decisions," *Psychological Science* 32, no. 6 (2021): 836–48.
15. Jessica Lasky-Fink, Carly D. Robinson, Hedy Nai-Lin Chang, and Todd Rogers, "Using behavioral insights to improve school administrative communications: The case of truancy notifications," *Educational Researcher* 50, no. 7 (2021): 442–50.
16. Ann Wylie, "What's the Latest U.S. Literacy Rate?" Wylie Communications, May 24, 2022, https://www.wyliecomm.com/2021/08/whats-the-latest-u-s-literacy-rate/.
17. "The State of Languages in the U.S.: A Statistical Portrait," American Academy of Arts and Sciences, December 7, 2016, https://www.amacad.org/publication/state-languages-us-statistical-portrait.

18. "Dyslexia FAQ," Yale Center for Dyslexia & Creativity, March 15, 2023, https://dyslexia.yale.edu/dyslexia/dyslexia-faq.
19. "Federal Plain Language Guidelines," Plain Language Action and Information Network, May 2011, https://www.plainlanguage.gov/media/FederalPLGuidelines.pdf.
20. Uri Benoliel and Samuel I. Becher, "The duty to read the unreadable," *Boston College Law Review* 60 (2019): 2255.
21. Alyxandra Cash and Hui-Ju Tsai, "Readability of the credit card agreements and financial charges," *Finance Research Letters* 24 (2018): 145–50; Paasche-Orlow, Taylor, and Brancati, "Readability standards for informed-consent forms"; Steven Walfish and Keely M. Watkins, "Readability level of health insurance portability and accountability act notices of privacy practices utilized by academic medical centers," *Evaluation & the Health Professions* 28, no. 4 (2005): 479–86.
22. Research on readability traditionally focuses on factors like the number of words per sentence, the number of syllables, and the sentence complexity. Our rules expand on these traditional definitions in order to develop actionable guidance for writers.
23. Though this quote is widely attributed to Twain on the internet, we could not find any credible sources noting when and where Twain said this.
24. "Google Books Ngram Viewer—Google Product," n.d., https://books.google.com/ngrams/.
25. Evan Halper, "These Word Cops Stand Guard to Keep Language Clear and Simple," *Los Angeles Times*, February, 19, 2021, https://www.latimes.com/politics/story/2021-02-19/enemies-opaque-deep-state-intolerant-of-government-incoherence.
26. Markowitz and Shulman, "The predictive utility of word familiarity."
27. David M. Markowitz, Maryam Kouchaki, Jeffrey T. Hancock, and Francesca Gino, "The deception spiral: Corporate obfuscation leads to perceptions of immorality and cheating behavior," *Journal of Language and Social Psychology* 40, no. 2 (2021): 277–96.

28. Daniel M. Oppenheimer, "Consequences of erudite vernacular utilized irrespective of necessity: Problems with using long words needlessly," *Applied Cognitive Psychology* 20, no. 2 (2006): 139–56.
29. "Submission Guidelines: Journal of Marketing," American Marketing Association, August 10, 2022, https://www.ama.org/submission-guidelines-journal-of-marketing/.
30. "Formatting Guide," *Nature*, https://www.nature.com/nature/for-authors/formatting-guide.
31. A. G. Sawyer, J. Laran, and J. Xu, "The readability of marketing journals: Are award-winning articles better written?" *Journal of Marketing* 72, no. 1 (2008): 108–17.
32. DuBay, "The Principles of Readability"; Edward Gibson, "Linguistic complexity: Locality of syntactic dependencies," *Cognition* 68, no. 1 (1998): 1–76.
33. Karolina Rudnicka, "Variation of sentence length across time and genre," in *Diachronic Corpora, Genre, and Language Change*, ed. Richard J. Whitt (Amsterdam: John Benjamins, 2018), 219–40.
34. Mark Liberman, Angela Duckworth, Lyle Ungar, Benjamin Manning, and Jordan Ellenberg, work in progress, 2023.
35. Lisa H. Trahan, Karla K. Stuebing, Merrill K. Hiscock, and Jack M. Fletcher, "The Flynn effect: A meta-analysis," *Psychological Bulletin* 140, no. 5 (2014): 1332, https://doi.org/10.1037/a0037173.
36. Liberman et al., work in progress, 2023.
37. Keith Rayner, Gretchen Kambe, and Susan A. Duffy, "The effect of clause wrap-up on eye movements during reading," *Quarterly Journal of Experimental Psychology: Section A* 53, no. 4 (2000): 1061–80; also Keith Rayner, Sara C. Sereno, Robin K. Morris, A. Rene Schmauder, and Charles Clifton Jr., "Eye movements and on-line language comprehension processes," *Language and Cognitive Processes* 4, no. 3–4 (1989): SI21–SI49.
38. George Washington, "First Inaugural Speech," April 30, 1789, National Archives, transcript, https://www.archives.gov/milestone-documents/president-george-washingtons-first-inaugural-speech;

Joseph R. Biden Jr., "Inaugural Address," January 20, 2021, White House Briefing Room, Speeches and Remarks, https://www.whitehouse.gov/briefing-room/speeches-remarks/2021/01/20/inaugural-address-by-president-joseph-r-biden-jr/.

39. Rachel Hvasta, "Ballot Measure Inaccessibility: Obscuring Voter Representation," February 9, 2020, https://www.americanbar.org/groups/crsj/publications/human_rights_magazine_home/voting-rights/ballot-measure-inaccessibility--obscuring-voter-representation/.

CHAPTER SIX: THIRD PRINCIPLE: DESIGN FOR EASY NAVIGATION

1. "Army Regulation 25–50: Information Management: Records Management: Preparing and Managing Correspondence," Department of the Army; Matthew Ström, "Bottom Line Up Front: Write to Make Decisions Faster," matthewstrom.com, May 17, 2020, https://matthewstrom.com/writing/bluf/.
2. Martin Baekgaard, Matthias Döring, and Mette Kjærgaard Thomsen, "It's not merely about the content: How rules are communicated matters to perceived administrative burden" (paper presented at the 2022 PMRA Conference in Phoenix, AZ, 2022).
3. Darren Grant, "The ballot order effect is huge: Evidence from Texas," *Public Choice* 172, no. 3 (2017): 421–42.
4. Kimberly Schweitzer and Narina Nuñez, "The effect of evidence order on jurors' verdicts: Primacy and recency effects with strongly and weakly probative evidence," *Applied Cognitive Psychology* 35, no. 6 (2021): 1510–22.
5. Jamie Murphy, Charles Hofacker, and Richard Mizerski, "Primacy and recency effects on clicking behavior," *Journal of Computer-Mediated Communication* 11, no. 2 (2006): 522–35.
6. Survey conducted with the Journalist's Resource, November 2022. N = 46,648.
7. "Monthly Due Date," plainlanguage.gov, n.d., https://www.plainlanguage.gov/examples/before-and-after/monthly-due-date/.

8. Alissa Fishbane, Aurelie Ouss, and Anuj K. Shah, "Behavioral nudges reduce failure to appear for court," *Science* 370, no. 6517 (2020): eabb6591.

CHAPTER SEVEN: FOURTH PRINCIPLE: USE ENOUGH FORMATTING BUT NO MORE

1. Paul Saenger, *Space Between Words: The Origins of Silent Reading* (Stanford, CA: Stanford University Press, 1997).
2. Online survey conducted on Prolific, December 2022.
3. "Full Disclosure," Federal Trade Commission, September 23, 2014, https://www.ftc.gov/business-guidance/blog/2014/09/full-disclosure.
4. Yonathan A. Arbel and Andrew Toler, "ALL-CAPS," *Journal of Empirical Legal Studies* 17, no. 4 (2020): 862–96.
5. Mary Beth Beazley, "Hiding in plain sight: 'Conspicuous type' standards in mandated communication statutes," *Journal of Legislation* 40 (2013): 1.
6. Beazley, "Hiding in plain sight," 1.
7. Though some laws do require all caps for making text conspicuous, using all caps does not necessarily satisfy legal requirements for clarity and conspicuousness in other contexts. In fact, the US Federal 9th Circuit Court wrote in *American General Finance, Inc. v. Bassett*, 285 F.3d 882 (2002), "Lawyers who think their caps lock keys are instant 'make conspicuous' buttons are deluded." See https://www.adamsdrafting.com/all-capitals/.
8. "Medicaid Eligibility," plainlanguage.gov, n.d., https://www.plainlanguage.gov/examples/before-and-after/medicaid-eligibility/.
9. Online survey conducted on MTurk, January 2023. N = 1,662.
10. Online survey conducted on MTurk, February 2021. N = 953.
11. Since this study was conducted for an academic paper on highlighting, we did not include similar conditions in which the irrelevant sentence was bolded or underlined. We predict the results would be the same, though: Readers would interpret the formatted words as the most important, and so they'd be prone to

skipping the rest of the passage and, in the process, miss out on the bonus.

12. Online survey conducted on MTurk, March 2021. N = 557.

CHAPTER EIGHT: FIFTH PRINCIPLE: TELL READERS WHY THEY SHOULD CARE

1. Elizabeth Louise Newton, "The rocky road from actions to intentions" (PhD diss., Stanford University, 1990).
2. Sharon E. Beatty and Scott M. Smith, "External search effort: An investigation across several product categories," *Journal of Consumer Research* 14, no. 1 (1987): 83–95; Hanjoon Lee, Paul M. Herr, Frank R. Kardes, and Chankon Kim, "Motivated search: Effects of choice accountability, issue involvement, and prior knowledge on information acquisition and use," *Journal of Business Research* 45, no. 1 (1999): 75–88.
3. Richard E. Petty and John T. Cacioppo, "Issue involvement can increase or decrease persuasion by enhancing message-relevant cognitive responses," *Journal of Personality and Social Psychology* 37, no. 10 (1979): 1915; Richard E. Petty, John T. Cacioppo, and Rachel Goldman, "Personal involvement as a determinant of argument-based persuasion," *Journal of Personality and Social Psychology* 41, no. 5 (1981): 847.
4. Lauren Marie Keane, "Sowing the seeds for grassroots growth: How recruitment appeals impact the calculus of citizen engagement" (PhD diss., University of Notre Dame, 2013).
5. Jacob D. Teeny, Joseph J. Siev, Pablo Briñol, and Richard E. Petty, "A review and conceptual framework for understanding personalized matching effects in persuasion," *Journal of Consumer Psychology* 31, no. 2 (2021): 382–414.

CHAPTER NINE: SIXTH PRINCIPLE: MAKE RESPONDING EASY

1. Brigitte C. Madrian and Dennis F. Shea, "The power of suggestion: Inertia in 401(k) participation and savings behavior," *Quarterly Journal of Economics* 116, no. 4 (2001): 1149–87.

2. Eric J. Johnson and Daniel G. Goldstein, "Defaults and donation decisions," *Transplantation* 78, no. 12 (2004): 1713–16.
3. Gretchen B. Chapman, Meng Li, Helen Colby, and Haewon Yoon, "Opting in vs opting out of influenza vaccination," *JAMA* 304, no. 1 (2010): 43–44.
4. Felix Ebeling and Sebastian Lotz, "Domestic uptake of green energy promoted by opt-out tariffs," *Nature Climate Change* 5, no. 9 (2015): 868–71.
5. Peter Bergman, Jessica Lasky-Fink, and Todd Rogers, "Simplification and defaults affect adoption and impact of technology, but decision makers do not realize it," *Organizational Behavior and Human Decision Processes* 158 (2020): 66–79.
6. Jeffrey R. Kling, Sendhil Mullainathan, Eldar Shafir, Lee C. Vermeulen, and Marian V. Wrobel, "Comparison friction: Experimental evidence from Medicare drug plans," *Quarterly Journal of Economics* 127, no. 1 (2012): 199–235.
7. Amos Tversky and Eldar Shafir, "Choice under conflict: The dynamics of deferred decision," *Psychological Science* 3, no. 6 (1992): 358–61; Sheena S. Iyengar and Mark R. Lepper, "When choice is demotivating: Can one desire too much of a good thing?" *Journal of Personality and Social Psychology* 79, no. 6 (2000): 995; Alexander Chernev, Ulf Böckenholt, and Joseph Goodman, "Choice overload: A conceptual review and meta-analysis," *Journal of Consumer Psychology* 25, no. 2 (2015): 333–58; Barry Schwartz, *The Paradox of Choice: Why More Is Less* (New York: Ecco, 2004).
8. Michael Lewis, "Obama's Way," *Vanity Fair*, September 11, 2012, https://www.vanityfair.com/news/2012/10/michael-lewis-profile-barack-obama.
9. John Beshears, James J. Choi, David Laibson, and Brigitte C. Madrian, "Simplification and saving," *Journal of Economic Behavior & Organization* 95 (2013): 130–45.
10. Jimmy Stamp, "Redesigning the Vote," *Smithsonian*, November 6, 2012, https://www.smithsonianmag.com/arts-culture/redesigning-the-vote-111423836/.

11. Jonathan N. Wand, Kenneth W. Shotts, Jasjeet S. Sekhon, Walter R. Mebane Jr., Michael C. Herron, and Henry E. Brady, "The butterfly did it: The aberrant vote for Buchanan in Palm Beach County, Florida," *American Political Science Review* 95, no. 4 (2001): 793–810; see also Craig R. Fox and Sim B. Sitkin, "Bridging the divide between behavioral science and policy," *Behavioral Science & Policy* 1, no. 1 (2015): 1–12.
12. Saurabh Bhargava and Dayanand Manoli, "Psychological frictions and the incomplete take-up of social benefits: Evidence from an IRS field experiment," *American Economic Review* 105, no. 11 (2015): 3489–529.
13. "EITC Participation Rate by States Tax Years 2012 through 2019," https://www.eitc.irs.gov/eitc-central/participation-rate-by-state/eitc-participation-rate-by-states.
14. The letters in the study called the earned income tax credit either the "Earned Income Credit" or "EIC."

CHAPTER TEN: TOOLS, TIPS, AND FAQS

1. Survey conducted with students in an executive education course, February 2021. N = 159.
2. Sionnadh Mairi McLean, Andrew Booth, Melanie Gee, Sarah Salway, Mark Cobb, Sadiq Bhanbhro, and Susan A. Nancarrow, "Appointment reminder systems are effective but not optimal: Results of a systematic review and evidence synthesis employing realist principles," *Patient Preference and Adherence* 10 (2016): 479–99.
3. Dean Karlan, Margaret McConnell, Sendhil Mullainathan, and Jonathan Zinman, "Getting to the top of mind: How reminders increase saving," *Management Science* 62, no. 12 (2016): 3393–411.
4. Peter Baird, Leigh Reardon, Dan Cullinan, Drew McDermott, and Patrick Landers, "Reminders to pay: Using behavioral economics to increase child support payments," *OPRE Report* 20 (2015).
5. Donald P. Green and Adam Zelizer, "How much GOTV mail is too much? Results from a large-scale field experiment," *Journal of Experimental Political Science* 4, no. 2 (2017): 107–18.

6. Cristian Pop-Eleches, Harsha Thirumurthy, James P. Habyarimana, Joshua G. Zivin, Markus P. Goldstein, Damien de Walque, Leslie MacKeen, et al., "Mobile phone technologies improve adherence to antiretroviral treatment in a resource-limited setting: A randomized controlled trial of text message reminders," *AIDS* 25, no. 6 (2011): 825–34.
7. Jessica Lasky-Fink and Todd Rogers, "Signals of value drive engagement with multi-round information interventions," *PLOS ONE* 17, no. 10 (2022): e0276072.
8. Elizabeth Linos, Allen Prohofsky, Aparna Ramesh, Jesse Rothstein, and Matthew Unrath, "Can nudges increase take-up of the EITC? Evidence from multiple field experiments," *American Economic Journal: Economic Policy* 14, no. 4 (2022): 432–52.
9. Dean Karlan and John A. List, "How can Bill and Melinda Gates increase other people's donations to fund public goods?" *Journal of Public Economics* 191 (2020): 104296.
10. Johanna Catherine Maclean, John Buckell, and Joachim Marti, "Information Source and Cigarettes: Experimental Evidence on the Messenger Effect," National Bureau of Economic Research, Working Paper No. 25632, March 2019. To learn much more on this, we also recommend Robert Cialdini's *Influence*.
11. Dan Bauman and Chris Quintana, "Drew Cloud Is a Well-Known Expert on Student Loans. One Problem: He's Not Real," *Chronicle of Higher Education*, April 24, 2018, https://www.chronicle.com/article/drew-cloud-is-a-well-known-expert-on-student-loans-one-problem-hes-not-real/.
12. Erica Dhawan, "Did You Get My Slack/Email/Text?" *Harvard Business Review*, May 7, 2021, https://hbr.org/2021/05/did-you-get-my-slack-email-text.
13. Jessica Lasky-Fink, Jessica Li, and Anna Doherty, "Reminder postcards and simpler emails encouraged more college students to apply for CalFresh," California Policy Lab, 2022.
14. Katerina Linos, Melissa Carlson, Laura Jakli, Nadia Dalma, Isabelle Cohen, Afroditi Veloudaki, and Stavros Nikiforos Spyrellis,

"How do disadvantaged groups seek information about public services? A randomized controlled trial of communication technologies," *Public Administration Review* 82, no. 4 (2022): 708–20.

15. Allison Dale and Aaron Strauss, "Don't forget to vote: Text message reminders as a mobilization tool," *American Journal of Political Science* 53, no. 4 (2009): 787–804.
16. Neil Malhotra, Melissa R. Michelson, Todd Rogers, and Ali Adam Valenzuela, "Text messages as mobilization tools: The conditional effect of habitual voting and election salience," *American Politics Research* 39, no. 4 (2011): 664–81.
17. Vote.org, "Increasing Voter Turnout—One Text at a Time," *Medium*, June 27, 2017, https://medium.com/votedotorg/increasing-voter-turnout-with-texts-voteorg-e38bd454bd64.
18. Ethan Pancer, Vincent Chandler, Maxwell Poole, and Theodore J. Noseworthy, "How readability shapes social media engagement," *Journal of Consumer Psychology* 29, no. 2 (2019): 262–70.
19. Gemma Fitzsimmons, Lewis T. Jayes, Mark J. Weal, and Denis Drieghe, "The impact of skim reading and navigation when reading hyperlinks on the web," *PLOS ONE* 15, no. 9 (2020): e0239134.
20. Justin Kruger, Nicholas Epley, Jason Parker, and Zhi-Wen Ng, "Egocentrism over e-mail: Can we communicate as well as we think?" *Journal of Personality and Social Psychology* 89, no. 6 (2005): 925–36.
21. Hannah Elizabeth Howman and Ruth Filik, "The role of emoticons in sarcasm comprehension in younger and older adults: Evidence from an eye-tracking experiment," *Quarterly Journal of Experimental Psychology* 73, no. 11 (2020): 1729–44.
22. Aiyana Ishmael, "Sending Smiley Emojis? They Now Mean Different Things to Different People," *Wall Street Journal*, August 9, 2021, https://www.wsj.com/articles/sending-a-smiley-face-make-sure-you-know-what-youre-saying-11628522840.
23. *Friel v. Dapper Labs, Inc. et al.*, 1:21-cv-05837-VM, page 46: https://assets.bwbx.io/documents/users/iqjWHBFdfxIU/rNL9SOS91Xgo/v0.

24. Claus-Peter Ernst and Martin Huschens, "Friendly, humorous, incompetent? On the influence of emoticons on interpersonal perception in the workplace," in *Proceedings of the 52nd Hawaii International Conference on System Sciences* (Grand Wailea, HI, 2019), http://hdl.handle.net/10125/59518.

CHAPTER ELEVEN: OUR WORDS, OUR SELVES

1. Stav Ziv, "Male and Female Co-Workers Switched Email Signatures, Faced Sexism," *Newsweek*, March 10, 2017, https://www.newsweek.com/male-and-female-coworkers-switched-email-signatures-faced-sexism-566507.
2. Ray Block Jr., Charles Crabtree, John B. Holbein, and J. Quin Monson, "Are Americans less likely to reply to emails from Black people relative to White people?" *Proceedings of the National Academy of Sciences* 118, no. 52 (2021): e2110347118.
3. Katherine L. Milkman, Modupe Akinola, and Dolly Chugh, "Temporal distance and discrimination: An audit study in academia," *Psychological Science* 23, no. 7 (2012): 710–17.
4. Daniel M. Butler and David E. Broockman, "Do politicians racially discriminate against constituents? A field experiment on state legislators," *American Journal of Political Science* 55, no. 3 (2011): 463–77.
5. Corrado Giulietti, Mirco Tonin, and Michael Vlassopoulos, "Racial discrimination in local public services: A field experiment in the United States," *Journal of the European Economic Association* 17, no. 1 (2019): 165–204.
6. Corinne A. Moss-Racusin, John F. Dovidio, Victoria L. Brescoll, Mark J. Graham, and Jo Handelsman, "Science faculty's subtle gender biases favor male students," *Proceedings of the National Academy of Sciences* 109, no. 41 (2012): 16474–79.
7. Rachele De Felice and Gregory Garretson, "Politeness at work in the Clinton email corpus: A first look at the effects of status and gender," *Corpus Pragmatics* 2 (2018): 221–42.
8. Carol Waseleski, "Gender and the use of exclamation points in computer-mediated communication: An analysis of exclamations

posted to two electronic discussion lists," *Journal of Computer-Mediated Communication* 11, no. 4 (2006): 1012–24.

9. Karina Schumann and Michael Ross, "Why women apologize more than men: Gender differences in thresholds for perceiving offensive behavior," *Psychological Science* 21, no. 11 (2010): 1649–55.
10. Robin Tolmach Lakoff, *Language and Woman's Place* (New York: Harper and Row, 1973).
11. Victoria Turk, "The Problem with Telling Women to Email Like Men," *Vice*, March 11, 2019, https://www.vice.com/en/article/8xyb5v/how-to-write-professional-work-email-women; Amelia Tait, "'Sorry for Bothering You!': The Emotional Labour of Female Emails," *New Statesman*, July 3, 2017, https://www.newstatesman.com/science-tech/2017/07/sorry-bothering-you-emotional-labour-female-emails.
12. Elizabeth Linos, Allen Prohofsky, Aparna Ramesh, Jesse Rothstein, and Matthew Unrath, "Can nudges increase take-up of the EITC? Evidence from multiple field experiments," *American Economic Journal: Economic Policy* 14, no. 4 (2022): 432–52; Elizabeth Linos, Jessica Lasky-Fink, Chris Larkin, Lindsay Moore, and Elspeth Kirkman, "The Formality Effect," HKS Working Paper No. RWP23-009 (2023).
13. Olivia M. Bullock and Austin Y. Hubner, "Candidates' use of informal communication on social media reduces credibility and support: Examining the consequences of expectancy violations," *Communication Research Reports* 37, no. 3 (2020): 87–98.
14. Anaïs Gretry, Csilla Horváth, Nina Belei, and Allard C. R. van Riel, "'Don't pretend to be my friend!' When an informal brand communication style backfires on social media," *Journal of Business Research* 74 (2017): 77–89.
15. Indrarini Laksmana, Wendy Tietz, and Ya-Wen Yang, "Compensation discussion and analysis (CD&A): Readability and management obfuscation," *Journal of Accounting and Public Policy* 31, no. 2 (2012): 185–203; Brian J. Bushee, Ian D. Gow, and Daniel J. Taylor, "Linguistic complexity in firm disclosures: Obfuscation or

information?" *Journal of Accounting Research* 56, no. 1 (2018): 85–121; John K. Courtis, "Annual report readability variability: Tests of the obfuscation hypothesis," *Accounting, Auditing & Accountability Journal* 11, no. 4 (1998): 459–72.

16. David M. Markowitz and Jeffrey T. Hancock, "Linguistic obfuscation in fraudulent science," *Journal of Language and Social Psychology* 35, no. 4 (2016): 435–45.

Index

About the Authors

Todd Rogers is a professor of public policy at Harvard University, where he has won teaching awards for the past seven consecutive years. He is a behavioral scientist and the cofounder of the Analyst Institute and EveryDay Labs. His opinion pieces have appeared in *The New York Times*, *The Washington Post*, the *Los Angeles Times*, and *Politico*, among other outlets.

Jessica Lasky-Fink is the research director at the People Lab, based at the Harvard Kennedy School. Her research focuses on improving the delivery of government programs and services.